# Hallow[ed]

## *Be Thy* Name

*Reflections on the Divine Name
in Sacred Scripture*

## Michael Lewis

Family Publications

Oxford

# Hallowed Be Thy Name

Reflections on the Divine Name
in Sacred Scripture

*Michael Lewis*

ISBN 1-871217-34-2

*Imprimatur:* Clyde Hughes Johnson STL
Chancellor of the Diocese of Menevia
17th July 2000

*Cover artwork:*
Icon of Christ, in ink
by Br Aidan Hart

*Cover background:*
Hebrew text of Exodus 3

Design by Richard J S Brown

Family Publications
77 Banbury Road, Oxford OX2 6LF
Tel: 01865 514408
www.familypublications.co.uk

Printed by Cromwell Press, Trowbridge, Wiltshire.

# Contents

## About the Author

Father Michael Lewis was born in London in 1947 and studied at St David's, Lampeter, and St John's Seminary, Wonersh. He was ordained a priest of the Diocese of Menevia at Rhyl in 1977, and has served at Rhyl, Flint, Burry Port and Wrexham. Since 1989, he has been Parish Priest of St Michael's, Brecon.

# Foreword

The Holy Father, Pope John Paul II, has constantly reminded the Church that Jesus was born 'an authentic son of Israel', and that we must appreciate this fact if we are to understand and hear the truth given to us in the Scriptures.

In this admirable book, Father Lewis, with his deep knowledge of Jewish spirituality, responds to this directive of the Holy Father, and reveals in a most illuminating way the significance of the Holy Name. In so doing, he gives the reader a deeper understanding of the Scriptures, and shows how the preparation for the Incarnation of the Word in the Old Testament is fulfilled in the New. Having read this book, I now find that whenever I encounter the Divine Name or the Holy Name of Jesus in the Scriptures, some aspect of the meaning of the Incarnation is brought to mind in a way that is spiritually most profitable.

At the same time, Father Lewis enables those who use the Jesus Prayer to do so with greater devotion, and to be grasped by its intensely rich meaning.

This is a book to be read slowly and meditatively. I am very glad to be able to commend it as a source of profound spiritual nourishment.

*Rt Rev & Rt Hon Mgr Graham Leonard*
*Witney, Oxon*

Jesu, the very thought of thee
With sweetness fills my breast;
But sweeter far thy face to see,
And in thy presence rest.

Nor voice can sing, nor heart can frame,
Nor can the memory find,
A sweeter sound than thy blest name,
O Saviour of mankind.

*Jesu Dulcis Memoria*

# Introduction

*Lord Jesus Christ, Son of God,*
*have mercy on me, a sinner*

In 1884, the anonymous *Candid Narratives of a Pilgrim to his Spiritual Father* was published in Kazan from a manuscript in the possession of an old abbot on Mount Athos. R M French, an assistant chaplain in Petrograd during the First World War, translated it into English as *The Way of a Pilgrim* in 1930. A sequel was published in Moscow in 1911 and this was translated into English, again by R M French, as *The Pilgrim Continues his Way*, which appeared in 1943. These two books possess a great charm, a lyrical and magical quality that breathes the simplicity of the Gospel, as they tell the story of the wanderings of the humble pilgrim through Russia in search of perpetual prayer, and of his many encounters on the way. Largely as a result of these two books, the Jesus Prayer became known outside of the Orthodox world, a process that had begun when the Russia of the pilgrim was engulfed by revolution, a cataclysmic event that resulted in the formation of a large Orthodox diaspora. The Prayer has radiated out throughout Christendom. Today, the Jesus Prayer is widely known and used by Catholics of the Roman Rite – it has even been incorporated into the New Rite of Penance as one of the optional acts of contrition – together with Anglicans, Lutherans and Free Churchmen.

There is now an extensive literature on the Jesus Prayer, with many excellent books readily available, and even web sites on the Internet. Although the Jesus Prayer is known and widely used far beyond Eastern Orthodoxy itself, the finest works on the Prayer still remain those by writers who are firmly rooted within the Eastern tradition. In writing this book on the Holy Name, I do not attempt to go over such ground at any length since it has already been far better covered than I could ever hope to do. Instead, my aim is to explore, in the light of Scripture and Tradition, something of the mystery and wonder of the Holy Name which is itself, of course, the very heart and foundation of the Jesus Prayer.

There are two underlying principles that are fundamental to my whole approach. The first principle is that the Bible *truly* is God's Word, not just a collection of 'spiritual' writings or religious texts, but God *really* speaking to us. As St Paul tells us: 'All scripture is inspired by God and is useful for teaching, for refutation, for correction, and for training in righteousness' [*2 Tim* 3:16].

Like a flash of lightning, one verse may shed light on another verse, perhaps written a thousand years later, because it is the same God who speaks to us through them all. Hence, God's words are truly spirit and life, timeless and always potent, capable of utterly transforming our lives – providing that, 'having heard the word with a good and noble heart', we 'keep it and bear fruit with patience' [*Lk* 8:15]. The Scriptures are indeed *Verbum Domini* – 'the word of the Lord' – and so, by definition, all Christian spirituality is a Biblical spirituality. The second underlying principle is a firm conviction that, if we are to understand the Scriptures, we need to remember always that Christianity is Jewish – although, of course, not exclusively so. In order to appreciate the full significance of much of what Christ did and said, it is necessary for us, as Gentile Christians, to make a certain leap of the imagination beyond the Anglo-Saxon picture of Christ that many of us still retain from Victorian religious art and Bible illustrations. In his Sacred Humanity, Christ was born as a Jew, lived, breathed and finally died and rose as a Jew, even though in Christ the barrier between Jew and Gentile has been torn down.

By God's plan and providence, the Church spread out and expanded from the Jewish world in which she was born, and her contact with the Hellenistic world was to be profoundly enriching and fruitful. None of this was by accident but by God's design and purpose, and those writers who argue for a 'pure' Christianity, purged of what they see as Greek accretions, are fundamentally mistaken. The Church is *incarnational* in time and space and cannot be frozen into any one particular cultural mode. But having said that, the far more pressing danger today is that we belittle or are even blind to the Jewishness of Christianity, and as a consequence end up with a distorted view of our own faith. We have to realise that, as Christ himself said, 'Salvation is of the Jews', and also, as St Paul wrote in *Romans*, that the Jews were entrusted with the word of God. This book will therefore draw deeply on Jewish sources and, as a result of this, parts of the material may at first sight appear unfamiliar to some readers. But it is all firmly rooted in Scripture as interpreted in the light of the Church's living tradition.

The wonderful beauty of the Scriptures and Tradition is that they constantly present us with 'new old' ways of contemplating the mystery of God's love for us as revealed in Christ. The more that we meditate on the Scriptures, the more we become aware of just how little we know. In God's word in Scripture, that which is eternal enters into time – and it is not by accident that the incarnate Word entered into time at a specific place and in a specific culture, that of first-century Palestine.

The Christ of faith and the Jesus of history are one. In order for us to learn how to pray, we need to look at Christ. Since he is the way, the truth and the life in all things, it follows that Christ's own example is normative for us as his disciples. He teaches us how to pray through the gift of his Spirit. If we are to understand something of the human prayer of Christ, then we have to place that prayer of his in its proper historical context, and this will enable us to discover how Christ understood his own mission.

Christ told us that he came to make known the Name of the Father. Just as to have seen Christ is to have seen the Father [*Jn* 12:45], so also to hallow the name of Jesus is to hallow the Name of the Father. The hallowing of God's Name lay at the very heart of Our Lord's life. In the *Torah*, the whole mission of Israel is summed up in the words of *Leviticus*:

> Thus you shall keep my commandments and observe them: I am the Lord. You shall not profane my holy name, that I may be sanctified among the people of Israel: I am the Lord; I sanctify you, I who brought you out of the land of Egypt to be your God: I am the Lord. [*Lev* 22:31–33]

The Messiah was a true son of David and he prayed as a Jew. In his prayer, as in all Jewish prayer down to our own day, the hallowing of the Name and the coming of the Kingdom are inextricably linked.

All of this has important consequences for us as Christians. As Pius XI observed, spiritually we are all Semites. We must be careful not to be Marcionite in our approach. Marcion was the second-century heretic who denied the continuity and unity of the Old and the New Testaments. He taught that the Old Testament was the work of an evil god and rejected it completely. Although no one now would subscribe to his views, many Christians act as if either consciously or unconsciously they believe that the Old Testament has in some way been replaced or made redundant by the New. Often a latent anti-Semitism lies behind such views. It is therefore imperative that we state the obvious over and over again. Not only was the Word made man, he was made a Jew.

Few popes have been more keenly aware of Our Lord's Jewish heritage than Pope John Paul II. In an address given to the Pontifical Biblical Commission on 11th April 1997, the Pope stated:

> Jesus' human identity is determined on the basis of his bond with the people of Israel, with the dynasty of David and his descent from Abraham. And this does not mean only a physical belonging. By taking part in the synagogue celebrations where the Old Testament texts were read and commented on, Jesus also came humanly to know these texts; he nourished his mind and his heart with them, using them in prayer and as an inspiration for his actions.
>
> Thus he became an authentic son of Israel, deeply rooted in his own people's long history... To deprive Christ of his relationship with the Old Testament is therefore to detach him from his roots and to empty his mystery of all meaning. Indeed, to be meaningful, the Incarnation had to be rooted in centuries of preparation. Christ would otherwise have been like a meteor that falls by chance to the earth and is devoid of any connection with human history.[1]

It is because Christ was born of a Jewish woman that he is an 'authentic son of Israel'. Jewish law defines a Jew as 'one born of a Jewish mother' and, in terms of transmitting the faith, the mother was then as she is now of key importance. During the hidden years in Nazareth, the child Jesus grew in wisdom and understanding; and the spirituality of Nazareth was very much a spirituality of the Name.

Mary was the perfect Daughter of Abraham. The *Catechism* observes:

> The Son of God who became the Son of the Virgin also learned to pray according to his human heart. He learns the formulas of prayer from his mother, who kept in her heart and meditated upon all the 'great things' done by the Almighty.[2]

At the Annunciation, her immediate response to the angelic message was to proclaim the holiness of God's Name. She would later have taught her son to revere God's holy Name and to remember always that, as a Jew, his whole life must be a *Kiddush ha-Shem*, a witness to and a sanctification of the Name of God.

This profound Jewish love of God's Name would have been something visible and palpable to the child Jesus from his earliest years. Take, for example, the *mezuzah* that would have been attached to the right-hand doorpost of the house of Joseph and Mary at Nazareth. The *mezuzah* consists of a small parchment script on which are inscribed verses taken from *Deuteronomy*, namely, the first two parts of the *Shema*, the great commandment. Carefully folded so that the part containing the Holy Name was uppermost, the parchment was placed in a small container affixed vertically to the doorpost.

Strictly speaking, the *Shema* is a command to obey rather than a prayer. The *Talmud* sees it, rather than the Decalogue, as containing the essence of the whole *Torah* [e.g. *Bera* 1.3c] and Jewish boys were taught it as soon as they could speak [*Sukk* 42a]. The words of the *Shema* read as follows:

> Hear, O Israel: the Lord our God, the Lord is One. Blessed be his name, whose glorious kingdom is for ever and ever. And thou shalt love the Lord thy God with all thine heart, and with all thy soul, and with all thy might. And these words which I command thee this day shall be upon thine heart: and thou shalt teach them diligently unto thy children, and shalt talk of them when thou sittest in thine house, and when thou walkest by the way, and when thou liest down, and when thou risest up. And thou shalt bind them for a sign upon thine hand, and they shall be for frontlet between thine eyes. And thou shalt write them upon the door posts of thy house and upon thy gates. [*Deut* 6:4–9]

Whenever an observant Jew enters or leaves the house, the custom is to touch the *mezuzah*, and then to kiss the fingers that had come into contact with the Holy Name, much as a Catholic might bless himself or herself from a holy water stoup by the door. Among Our Lord's earliest memories would have been those of Mary and Joseph holding Him up so that he could reach to touch the *mezuzah*.

It was against such a background of piety and devotion that the Messiah grew to maturity. There was the regular rhythm and pattern of the worship of the synagogue where the liturgy continually celebrated the holiness of the Name. Both at the synagogue and at home, Christ learned to know, love and to make the Psalms his own, the Psalms which over and over again praise the power and the glory of the Name: 'Blessed be the Name of the Lord, now and for ever'. For many of the great festivals, especially for Passover, Christ went on pilgrimage to the Temple in Jerusalem, the dwelling place on earth of the Name. And he would have said after the first verse of the *Shema*, 'Blessed be the name of his glorious Kingdom for ever and ever', words that expressed all the longing of Israel for freedom and deliverance. We cannot separate Our Lord from his Jewish spiritual identity.

This Old Testament devotion to the Name comes to its fulfilment and perfection in the New. It has continued to grow and flourish in Judaism down the centuries, becoming one of the chief hallmarks of Jewish mysticism. Although much of this Jewish tradition is not as well known to Christians as it deserves to be, it can help to illuminate much that is in the New Testament, reflecting as it does the fruit of the prayerful meditation and study of countless scholars upon the Hebrew Scriptures. Jewish exegesis and commentary provide an extremely valuable tool in enabling us to appreciate those Scriptures in their proper cultural and religious milieu. As we reflect on the Name, we remember that Christ came not to abolish the old revelation but to bring it to complete fulfilment, and that when he prayed to his Father, he prayed as a Jew.

---

1 Pope John Paul II, 'Old Testament essential to know Jesus', in *L'Osservatore Romano*, 23 April 1997, N°. 17 (1488) ed. 2.
2 *Catechism of the Catholic Church*, para. 2599.

# The Name that is Above All Other Names

*Therefore My people shall know My name; therefore they*
*shall know in that day that I am He who speaks:*
*'Behold, it is I'.*  [*Is* 52:6]

Every day of our lives we pray that the Name may be 'hallowed', and yet the very familiarity of these words means that we so easily take them for granted. We need to explore some of the wonders of the Holy Name and to meditate on the wealth of meaning that lies in these well-known words. Perhaps the best starting-point for these reflections is to quote some of the most astounding words ever written on the Name of Jesus. These words come from the *Catechism of the Catholic Church* and are breathtaking in their implications. They come as a conclusion to a discussion of the various titles and names of Our Lord:

> But the one name that contains everything is the one that the Son of God received in his incarnation: JESUS. The divine name may not be spoken by human lips, but by assuming our humanity the Word of God hands it over to us and we can invoke it: 'Jesus', 'YHWH saves'. The name 'Jesus' contains all: God and man and the whole economy of creation and salvation. To pray 'Jesus' is to invoke him and to call him within us. His name is the only one that contains the presence it signifies. Jesus is the Risen One, and whoever invokes the name of Jesus is welcoming the Son of God who loved him and who gave himself up for him.[1]

What strikes us immediately and forcefully is that the language used is sacramental language, almost as if the writer were speaking of the Eucharist itself – the name 'Jesus' contains all, the presence of Jesus himself and the whole mystery of salvation. To pray in the Name of Jesus is to have access to the Father and it is only by the Holy Spirit that such prayer is possible. For those who call on Him in humility of heart, the Name brings into effect what it signifies – the saving presence of Jesus.

These inspiring words of the *Catechism* contain a great hope for us. The prospect opens for us of a way of prayer that is readily accessible to all, a simple way of prayer that is capable, with God's grace, of utterly transforming our spiritual lives. The Name of Jesus is our interface with the Lord himself.

But why is the Name of Jesus the name that contains everything and possesses such unique power? It is certainly not through any magical property of the Name itself. Indeed, the name 'Jesus' (*Yeshua* or *Iesous*) was a common one amongst Jews until the second century, when it fell into disuse, largely as a result of its association with the Christian profession of faith in Jesus as Messiah. Although the name is not used as a Christian name in Anglo-Saxon countries, it is so used in the Hispanic world. There is nothing innately mystical in the Name itself. What matters is the link with the Son of God himself.

We can arrive at an answer to the question only by keeping always sharply in focus the fundamental truth that the One who bears the Name, Jesus, the Son of Mary, is both fully God and fully Man. Jesus is the Name of the Messiah, the Name of the Word made flesh. The key passage is to be found in St Paul's letter to the Church in Philippi. Probably quoting from a very early Christian hymn, Paul says of the Messiah:

> who, being in the form of God,
> did not consider it robbery to be equal with God,
> but made himself of no reputation,
> taking the form of a bondservant,
> and coming in the likeness of men.
> And being found in appearance as a man,
> He humbled himself
> and became obedient to the point of death,
> even the death of the cross.
> Therefore God also has highly exalted Him
> and given Him the name which is above every name,
> that at the name of Jesus every knee should bow,
> of those in heaven, and of those on earth,
> and of those under the earth,
> and that every tongue should confess
> that Jesus Christ is Lord,
> to the glory of God the Father. [*Phil* 2:6–11]

As a divine person, Christ never ceases for one moment to possess the divine nature. He empties himself by assuming our human nature, not by ceasing to be God. Having been made truly man, Christ comes in the likeness of men and appears among us as all men are. He comes not as the King of Kings, surrounded by legions of angels, but enters the world as a tiny Jewish child who, on the eighth day at his '*berit milah*', his circumcision, receives the name of Jesus, a name chosen by God himself. Christ takes the form of a bondservant. What was invisible is now visible, what was intangible can now be touched, what was inaudible can now be heard. Isaiah's passionate prayer 'O that he would rend the heavens open and come down' has now been answered in the presence among us of the Man of sorrows, acquainted with grief. The Name that cannot be spoken by human lips can now be invoked by all.

In his sacred humanity, from Bethlehem to Calvary, Christ reveals his perfect humility and obedience, culminating in death on the cross. By accepting the shame of death on a cross, he is highly exalted by God and given the name that is above all other names and, having suffered in his Sacred Humanity, the risen and exalted Christ is to be forever glorified in that Humanity. The flesh of Christ is the hinge upon which hangs our salvation. This exaltation of Christ necessarily includes the exaltation of his human name.

The name of Jesus ('Yahweh saves' or 'Yahweh is salvation') states both who he is and what he does. He is called 'Jesus' for 'He will save his People from their sins', and he is the one who will reign over the House of Jacob forever, and of whose kingdom there will be no end. Just as the humanity of Christ is to be adored because the person who assumed it is a divine person, so the name of Jesus is to be hallowed because it is the Name of the One who is Lord: *Kyrios* and *Adonai*.

A second question has to be asked. What is the Name that is above all other names? In *Isaiah* 45:23, Yahweh says

> By myself I swear, uttering my just decree
> and my unalterable word:
> To me every knee shall bend;
> by me every tongue shall swear.

The one who speaks is the 'I Am', Yahweh, who spoke out of the burning bush at the dawn of Israel's redemption. In the Greek version of the Old Testament, the Greek 'Kyrios' (Lord) is used to translate the Hebrew YHWH but 'Kyrios' is not as such the divine Name in itself.

From the whole flow of the passage, it is clear that the Name that Christ receives cannot simply be the divine title of 'Lord', which is properly speaking an attribute rather than a name. It is at the name of Jesus that the knee of every creature must bend, and at the name of Jesus that every tongue must confess that Jesus Christ is Lord. What Paul has in mind is the ineffable Name of God itself which is the Name that is above all other names, the Name that denotes God's own inner being, the divine essence itself, He Who Is. As such, this Name is beyond all human speech. But, as is evident from the context and thrust of the words of the hymn, the human Name of Jesus is in some transcendent manner united to that mysterious Name. What is said of Yahweh and his Name can be said of Jesus and his Name.

After celebrating Christ's perfect obedience even unto death on a cross, the hymn continues in a tone of exultant ecstasy: it is because of this perfect obedience that God has greatly exalted Christ and bestowed on him the Name that is above every name. A clear link is made between 'Lord' and 'Name', but the two are not, strictly speaking, synonymous, and the equality between the Name of Jesus and the Name of God does not mean that they are therefore identical or interchangeable. It is because Jesus has received the Name that is above every other Name, that at the Name of Jesus every tongue must confess that Jesus is Lord.

There is an immediate difficulty if we conclude without qualification that the Name of Jesus is, itself, the Name above all other names. As a matter of historical record the Messiah was given the human name of 'Jesus' at a specific historical moment – the Annunciation – that is, at a moment in time that preceded his Glorification. Before the revelation of the Name in time, God knew the Name of Jesus from all eternity as the Name of the Messiah, the Name of Immanuel, God-with-us.

Paul states that it was at the exaltation that God gave Jesus the Name that is above all other names. It is also evident that, for Paul, the divine will expressed in this gift of the Name is precisely that the Name of Jesus should receive the same cult as the Name of YHWH. But the exaltation is not the *giving* of divinity to Christ because, as God, Christ is eternally and consubstantially divine. From all eternity, the Son of God is 'He Who Is', and thus the exaltation is the *manifestation* of what had been hidden from all eternity. Perhaps Paul's thought can be best understood in the context of what might be termed a Christian *Shema*: 'Hear, O Israel: the Lord our God, YHWH and Jesus, the Lord is One.'

Here, we must bear in mind, Paul is not writing systematic theology, and we should remember his rabbinic training. One of the great concerns of the Rabbis was the whole question of determining the rules governing biblical exegesis. In the first half of the second century, Rabbi Ishmael formulated the classical expression of these rules in his thirteen principles, but earlier Rabbis had already substantially anticipated his work. If we apply one of his principles to the Philippian hymn, then the meaning of the whole of the passage can be interpreted as being derived from a statement made later in the passage. This hermeneutical principle reflects the parallelism of sense that is such a characteristic of Hebrew poetry, notably of the Psalms, where a word or words in one line have their parallel in another, sometimes by way of antithesis or of partial repetition of one line leading to a new affirmation.

As we have seen, the whole passage is concerned with the exaltation of the Man Jesus, and culminates with the statement that Jesus Christ is Lord, to the glory of God the Father. God has given Jesus the Messiah the name that is above all other Names in order that 'at the Name of Jesus every knee should bow ... and every tongue confess that Jesus the Messiah is Lord'. The giving of the Name is part of the whole process of the exaltation of the Sacred Humanity of Our Lord, a process that necessarily must include the exaltation of the human Name of Jesus. The exaltation of the Messiah and the exaltation of the Name of the Messiah are insepararably linked.

For Paul, the Name of Jesus, the Name of the glorified and risen Christ, and the Name that is above all other names, the Tetragrammaton, are both one and yet distinct. As Paul says in *Colossians* 1:15, Christ is 'the image of the invisible God, the firstborn of all creation'. The name of Jesus is the image of the Ineffable Name, just as Jesus is the Image of the Invisible God. Paul would have been familiar with the Rabbinic tradition that the Name of the Messiah was one of the secrets known to God before the very beginning of creation itself. This thought is also probably to be found in *The Odes of Solomon*, an ecstatic collection of Christian hymns of Syriac origin, dating from the close of the first century:

> The Son of the most High appeared
> in the perfection of the Father.
> and light dawned from the Word
> that was before time in him.
> The Messiah in truth is one.
> And he was known before the foundations of the world,
> that he might give life to persons forever
> by the truth of his Name.[2]

Just as *Revelation* speaks of the Lamb as having been slain from the foundation of the world [13:8], so too we can see the Name of Jesus as a divine Name from before the creation itself and the Incarnation itself. [3]

We recall Christ's prayer in John's Gospel: ' "Now My soul is troubled, and what shall I say? 'Father, save Me from this hour'? But for this purpose I came to this hour. Father, glorify Your name." Then a voice came from heaven, saying, "I have both glorified it and will glorify it again" ' [*Jn* 12:27–28]. The glorification of Christ ushers in the new age when the name of Jesus can be invoked. As Christ says to the Apostles on the eve of his glorification: 'Until now you have not asked anything in my name; ask and you will receive, so that your joy may be complete' [*Jn* 16:24]. The Church now lives in the age of the joy of the Name.

---

1 *Catechism of the Catholic Church*, London, 1999; para. 2666.

2 *Ode 41* in J H Charlesworth [ed.], *The Old Testament Pseudepigrapha*, Vol. 2, London, 1985; p.770.

3 The question of the eternity of the Name of Jesus is related to that of the absolute priority of Jesus Christ over all things and the whole relationship of creation and redemption. Q.v. F-X Durrwell, *The Mystery of Christ and the Apostolate*, London, New York, 1972; pp. 19–41.

# The Word and the Name

*He was clothed with a robe dipped in blood, and his name
is called The Word of God.*   [*Rev* 19:13]

At the dawn of all, God spoke and everything sprang into being. By his
Word, God made all things. All that was, is now, or is yet to be, God
created in, through, and for, his beloved Son; and the last of his works is
man, the priest and steward of creation. You and I exist simply because
God is good. Every moment of our lives he invites us to be plunged into
the abyss of love that is the Trinity, to drink freely of the water of life, to
be made one with Him.

Our very existence as creatures is defined by our absolute dependence
upon God and yet we, who are nothingness, are called to share in the
divine nature itself, as sparks within the fire. Philaret, the great nineteenth-
century Metropolitan of Moscow, expressed it beautifully:

> All creatures are balanced upon the creative word of God, as if
> upon a bridge of diamond; above them is the abyss of the divine
> infinitude, below them that of their own nothingness.[1]

By reason alone, we can indeed know much of God from the world that
he has made, but it is God's revelation of himself that transforms our
understanding. We enter into a world of dialogue, of 'I' and 'Thou,' a
world of names. Our God is the living God of Abraham, Isaac and Jacob,
who reveals to us the wonder of his love by telling us his Name. The
Absolute of the philosopher, the one Being who alone exists of himself
and upon whom all other creatures depend, is one and the same God who
makes his Name known to us that we might know and love him.

The single utterance of the Father is his Word, his only begotten Son,
and the Word that is the perfect image of his Being. That same Word,
made flesh, has a name, and that name is Jesus. In Him dwells the fullness
of the Godhead; and in the mystery of Jesus, the whole mystery of our
salvation is contained.

The words of Sacred Scripture are an icon of the Word spoken by the
Father. Just as in the tradition of the Church, sacred art is much more than

art with a religious theme, but rather a manifestation into the visible order of invisible realities, so the words of Scripture are much more than a collection of religious writings. They are a manifestation in human language of the eternal Word that is spoken by the Father in the silence of eternity. More than anything else in the Church today, we need to recapture a visionary approach to the Scriptures, and to take seriously those words that we say at the end of each reading at Mass, 'This is the word of the Lord.'

To compose the books of Sacred Scripture, God chose certain men and, as we read in *The Dogmatic Constitution on Divine Revelation* of the Second Vatican Council, all the while that he employed them in this task, he made full use of their powers and faculties so that, though he acted in them and by them, it was as true authors that they consigned to writing whatever he wanted written, and no more.[2] It is self-evident that the writings contained in Sacred Scripture came into existence at specific moments of time; but that is not the whole story. The divinely revealed realities contained and presented in the text pre-existed in the mind of God before they were ever set down in human writing.

In this sense, we can indeed speak of the Scriptures as having existed from all eternity in the mind of God, as the words of the Word. Just as the tiniest visible fragment of the Blessed Sacrament surpasses in value the whole of creation because it is Christ himself, so a single verse of Scripture, if only we had the faith to realise it, surpasses in value the whole of human literature. Writing of the great saints of the early Church, the Orthodox theologian Paul Evdokimov stated:

> While reading Scripture, the Fathers read not words, but the living Christ, and Christ spoke to them. They consumed words in the manner of the Eucharistic bread and wine, and the word appeared to them in its Christ dimension.[3]

Even before the Incarnation, the Word of God took a human form in the human language of the Scriptures, the means by which the eternal Word that transcends all human thought becomes capable of being communicated to his creation. Both human and divine, the Scriptures are, as it were, a sacrament of our salvation, a presence of Christ in our midst. The uncreated light shines through the prism of human language, and in the myriad glories of the rainbow that shine forth, we are able to perceive the light. We are what we eat, and the story of our salvation is the story of God feeding us with his Word:

> Your words were found, and I ate them, and Your word was to me the joy and rejoicing of my heart; for I am called by Your name, O Lord God of hosts. [*Jer* 15:16]

God created man with a hunger for his Word, for the words of eternal life. Man is a hunger for the word of God. This hunger is part of what defines us as human beings and differentiates us from the animals. Man does not live on bread alone but on every word that comes from the mouth of God. From the first word of creation by which he called us into existence, through all the words of revelation, culminating in the Eucharist, the mystery of God's loving plan of redemption is the mystery by which he feeds us with those words.

All of this should lead us to find in sacred scripture the living spring of our spirituality. The word of God is not a lifeless word – it is the all-powerful word by which creation came to be; it is alive and active, vibrant with light and glory. In this, we can learn from our elder brothers, the Jews, with their passionate love of the Scripture. The Evangelists speak of Our Lord as a Rabbi. As a Rabbi, Our Lord was versed not just in the *Tanach*, the Hebrew Scriptures, but also the *Mishnah*, the Oral Law. An understanding of the Jewish background to his teaching will enrich our insight into his words and message.

If we are to explore the theme of the Name of God in sacred Scripture and to appreciate something of its meaning, we must never forget that God's revelation is a seamless unity. Our ears must become attuned to the words of Scripture, its music and its rhythms. When we listen to its words, we should do so with awareness that it takes time and prayer to appreciate its treasures. Those words, as contained in the sacred text, are largely in Hebrew, a language which is, above all, the language of the concrete, of the physical, of the dynamic and vital.

If we bring to the Old Testament the same linguistic associations and assumptions that we bring to a modern English text, then we run the very real risk of obscuring the full force of that word. Here, of course, the fidelity of any translation to the inspired text is of crucial importance.

The curious fashion of our own day, for translators to remould God's words into our own image and likeness, is ultimately blasphemous. This is reflected in certain modern translations of the Scriptures based on the theory of 'dynamic equivalence', whereby the translator seeks to convey the meaning or the sense of the words of the sacred text rather than to provide an exact and precise translation of the actual text. Although there may be a few instances where this is necessary for understanding, 'dynamic equivalence' can become little more than a justification for paraphrase, inspired by a desire to 'revise' the text in the light of contemporary concerns. The obsession with gender-free language is an example of this. More generally, the result is a 'dumbing down' of the richness and subtlety of the text. We need to have the humility to recognise that God chooses, better than we can, the saving words that express his revelation of himself.[4]

We need to discover the truth of Pius XI's dictum that 'spiritually we are all Semites', and this will involve a readiness on our part to open ourselves to God's word in a new and fresh way. St Paul tells us that the Jews were entrusted with the very words of God [*Rom* 3:2] and, down the centuries, the Jews have treasured those words, above all the *Torah*, the first five books of Sacred Scripture, which they call the Tree of Life.

How profound is that Jewish reverence for Scripture, is readily apparent to anyone who visits a synagogue. In every synagogue, the *Torah* is stored in an ark, the *Aron Hakodesh*, a finely-worked cabinet upon a platform. Like the traditional practice with the Christian altar, the Ark is normally located by the east wall and orientated towards Jerusalem. A curtain screens the Ark, and placed close by it is an ever-burning light, the *ner tamid*. The light is a symbol of the light of God's word and also of the divine presence, the *Shekhinah*, a word that means literally 'dwelling' or 'resting,' referring to 'God with us' as distinct from 'God in himself.'

The *Torah* scroll itself is regarded as being so sacred that it may not be touched directly by the human hand. When it is read aloud, a special pointer, a *yad* (a rod with a sculptured hand at one end) is used to guide the eye and to mark the place. Should the scroll or any book containing the sacred text become worn by age, it is not lawful to throw it away: it must be buried in a cemetery. Should a *Torah* scroll be dropped by accident, all male members of the congregation present are bound to atone by fasting for twenty-four hours. Although, of course, the *Torah* scroll is not worshipped, it is nonetheless treated with a respect and veneration that is reminiscent of Catholic devotion to the reserved Sacrament.

The Rabbis taught that when two or three were gathered to study the *Torah*, they were in the presence of the *Shekhinah*. Some Jewish mystics maintained that the whole of the *Torah* constituted the name of God. Obviously, the Name of God is not here a name in the sense of a word that can be pronounced. Rather the *Torah* as 'Name' is seen as an expression in time and space, in as far as it can be revealed, of the transcendent Being and Power of God, that is concentrated in his 'Name.'

In the *Talmud*, it is said that before the creation of the universe, the *Torah* was with God and was written in white fire on black fire. Every letter was held to contain the most wondrous of mysteries, and yet the greatest of mysteries, the infinite meaning of the *Torah*, lay in the ocean of whiteness that surrounds the black letters, the meaning of which will only be understood in the world to come.

Such thoughts plunge us into prayer. All Scripture is an encounter with the saving Christ. Scripture is endowed with saving grace because, through human words, the Father communicates his Son to us in the Spirit. The words of eternal life mirror in time the very life of the Trinity itself, and God's communication of himself to us. Everything goes out from the Father through the Word in the Holy Spirit, and, at the Incarnation, returns to the Father in the Incarnate Word by the power of the Holy Spirit. By uniting human nature to his Word, the Incarnation, the whole of creation which went out from God returns to God, joined to him in the sacred humanity of the Incarnate Word. Scripture is indeed full of grace. In it, the Father reaches out to man through the Son to draw man to himself in the unity of the Spirit.

With the coming of the Incarnate Word, mankind has entered that world that is to come, although we still await its perfect fulfilment and realisation when Christ will return in glory at the end of time. Already we live in the age when the white fire of not just the *Torah* but of the whole of the Scriptures is before us. As the *Catechism* says,

> Through all the words of Sacred Scripture, God speaks only one single Word, his one Utterance in whom he expresses himself completely: 'You recall that one and the same Word of God extends throughout Scripture, that is one and the same Utterance that

resounds in the mouths of all the sacred writers, since he who was in the beginning God with God has no need of separate syllables; for he is not subject to time.'[5]

For this reason, the Church has always venerated the Scripture as she venerates the Lord's Body. In Sacred Scripture, the Church constantly finds her nourishment and her strength, for she welcomes it not as a human word, 'but as what it really is, the word of God'. In the sacred books, the Father who is in heaven comes lovingly to meet his children, and talks with them.

In the encounter between God and man, names are spoken and exchanged. However, these are names which have a much deeper significance than human speech can convey. Just as to have seen Christ is to have seen the Father, so to hear the name of Jesus with faith is to hear the name of the Father. From the beginning, man has sought to know God and to know his Name, but the Name of God, the ineffable Name, is not an attribute of God: it is God himself. The whole story of revelation is essentially the story of God's progressive disclosure of his Name, his innermost being, to man, and of how we are saved by that Name.

---

1 Quoted by V Lossky in *The Mystical Theology of the Eastern Church,* London, 1957; p. 92.

2 *Dei Verbum* 11.

3 Quoted by T   pidlík, *The Spirituality of the Christian East: A Systematic Handbook,* Kalamazoo, Michigan, 1986; p.6.

4 Compare, for example, the approach to Scripture found in some of our freer 'translations' to that of the Lithuanian mystic Alexander Susskind of Grodno (d. 1793) who wrote thus : '...a man should rejoice exceedingly over our marvellous holy *Torah* and with great rapture he should say to himself many times: "The wonders of God. The wonders of God," amazed at the thought that hidden mysteries are hinted at in every single point of our holy *Torah*, in every letter, every vowel point, every musical notation, heaps upon heaps of such tremendous mysteries that even the holy angels are incapable of grasping fully even a single letter of our holy *Torah*.' (Louis Jacobs (ed.), *The Jewish Mystics*, London, 1976; p. 189)

5 *Catechism of the Catholic Church*, para. 102–4.

# The Revelation of the Name

*Then Moses said to God, 'Indeed, when I come to the*
*children of Israel and say to them, "The God of your*
*fathers has sent me to you", and they say to me, "What is*
*His name?", what shall I say to them?' [Ex 3:13]*

To the modern Western mind, personal names are often little more than
mere designations or labels, arbitrary things, badges that can be attached
or detached at will. We regard names as externals, superficial things, a
part of the world of appearance that we perceive, rather than relating to
how the world actually is, that world of the thing-in-itself which Kant
held lies beyond our experience. The highly influential Swiss linguist
Saussure saw language itself as fundamentally a structure of signs with
no inherent meaning in isolation from the system as a whole. A name
would be a linguistic sign devoid of any essential meaning save that which
is accorded it by convention and common consent. On this philosophy, a
rose by any other name would indeed smell as sweet. There is a complete
dichotomy between language and reality, between the signifier and the
signified, and between the sound or the written mark and the person in
mind. Language is reduced to the level of a game of chess.

Such a way of thinking would have seemed almost incomprehensible
to the people of the Bible. Shakespeare's question 'What's in a name?'
would have puzzled an Israelite, because, for the Hebrew mind, the name
and the person were one: 'as his name is, so is he.' [*1 Sam* 25:25]. The
name is a manifestation of the person named, a part of them, a potent
symbol that not only expresses but, in a mysterious way, is actually charged
with the being of the person it names. It is an expression of the underlying
reality of the person named. In the Scriptures, names convey much of the
significance of what we understand by 'person', and thus, by metonymy,
names are often used for the person, such as 'through his name' meaning
'through him'.

The Bible sees a man's soul as present in his name, and thus to reveal
one's name is to reveal oneself. Names are analogous to a sacrament:
they make the person present. There are numerous Scriptural incidences

of a person's reluctance to disclose his name to an enquirer. Addressing the angel of the Lord, the Lord himself, Jacob asks: ' "Tell me your name, I pray." And He said, "Why is it that you ask about my name?" And he blessed him there.' [*Gen* 32:29] Similarly, Manoah asks the Angel of the Lord, ' "What is your name, that when Your words come to pass we may honour You?" And the Angel of the Lord said to him, "Why do you ask my name, seeing it is wonderful?" ' [*Judg* 13:17–18]. Both are very archaic passages, and the underlying thought is that knowledge of the name bestows a power on the person who knows the name.

The *Catechism of the Catholic Church* expresses beautifully the whole Semitic theology of the Name:

> God revealed himself to his people Israel by making his Name known to them. A name expresses a person's essence and identity, and the meaning of this person's life. God has a name; he is not an anonymous force. To disclose one's name is to make oneself known to others; in a way it is to hand oneself over by becoming accessible, capable of being known more intimately and addressed personally.[1]

God makes the fundamental revelation of his Name for both Old and New Covenants to Moses at the theophany of the burning bush. In the great Name revealed to Moses on the eve of the Exodus and the Covenant of Sinai, God communicates the whole inner meaning of the faith of the Old Testament and the promise of the coming of the Saviour.

We recall the scene. Tending the flock of his father-in-law Jethro in the wilderness, Moses leads them to Horeb, the mountain of God. Out of the midst of a burning thorn bush, the angel of the Lord appears to him in a flame of fire that did not consume the bush. Moses turns aside to see this wonder and God, seeing him turn aside, calls him twice by name. His reply to God's call is simply to say 'Here I am,' the only response man can make in the presence of the Holy, the response of a child to the summons of its father or mother. It is the 'I' responding to the 'thou' as Moses encounters the God who calls him by name.

God warns Moses not to approach too close and tells him to remove his shoes for he is standing on holy ground. This sense of the numinous is an essential part of the theophany, for what is man before God? Moses hides his face for he is afraid to look at God. Then the great revelation of the Name begins as God promises salvation for captive Israel but first he reveals himself as the God of Amram:

> So when the Lord saw that he turned aside to look, God called to him from the midst of the bush and said, 'Moses, Moses!' And he said, 'Here I am'. Then he said, 'Do not draw near this place. Take your sandals off your feet, for the place where you stand is holy ground'. Moreover he said, 'I am the God of your father, the God of Abraham, the God of Isaac, and the God of Jacob'. And Moses hid his face, for he was afraid to look upon God. [*Ex* 3:4–6]

The Lord is not the Absolute of the philosophers, an unknown God, but the God of human beings, of great and small alike. He is the God of Amram, Moses's father, an otherwise insignificant member of the tribe of Levi that will later be associated with the priesthood. God reveals himself as the God who had covenanted himself with the great Patriarchs, and also the God of the obscure Amram whose name appears only once in the whole of Scripture.

Above all, God is the God who speaks to man, addresses him by word. In man's past, he is the God of Amram, Abraham, Isaac and Jacob. In man's present, he is the God who tells Moses that he has seen the misery and affliction of his people in bondage in Egypt. Now he has come down to deliver them out of the hands of the Egyptians. In man's future, he is the God who will bring the people of Israel out of Egypt 'to a very broad land, a land flowing with milk and honey'. This same God of the Patriarchs will be with Moses as his instrument to free his people. God names himself as the God who is, who was and will be with his people. In thus revealing his Name, his intimate nature, to Moses, God is revealing his mercy for his people.

On Sinai, the people of Israel will serve the Lord. At Sinai, God will give the law to the People whom he has called and enter into covenant with them. There the Israelites will become the *Qahal*, the assembly of the people. In the *Septuagint*, the Greek translation of the Old Testament, *Qahal* is translated as *Ekklesia* – 'Church'. From the great revelation of the Name will spring the revelation of the Law. The people will hear the Word, be formed by that Word and become the People of the Name. Israel's vocation will be to witness to that Name and to bear its stamp, sharing in all the depth of relationship with God that the Name implies.

Then Moses asked God:

> 'Indeed, when I come to the children of Israel and say to them, "The God of your fathers has sent me to you", and they say to me, "What is his name?", what shall I say to them?' And God said to Moses, 'I am who I am' [*Ehyeh Asher Ehyeh*]. And he said, 'Thus you shall say to the children of Israel, "I am has sent me to you".' Moreover God said to Moses, 'Thus you shall say to the children of Israel: "The Lord [YHWH], God of your fathers, the God of Abraham, the God of Isaac, and the God of Jacob, has sent me to you. This is my name forever, and this is my memorial to all generations. I am the God of your fathers, the God of Abraham, the God of Isaac, and the God of Jacob." ' And he said, 'Say this to the people of Israel, "I am [*Ehyeh*] has sent me to you" '. [*Ex* 3:13–15]

The divine Name has two forms. The first – '*Ehyeh*' ('I Am') – is used when God himself is speaking. '*Ehyeh*' is the *Qal* imperfect, first person singular, of the root '*hyh*' or '*hwh*', 'to be'. When others speak of God, the third person singular form is used, 'YHWH', that is 'He Is' or 'He Who Is'. Both forms are derived from the same root '*hyh*' or '*hwh*'. The first person singular can also be translated as 'I will be what I will be', and this was the translation favoured by Rashi, the greatest of all Jewish commentators. It is an existential answer, an answer that comes out of the heart of the divine fire of God's love itself. The 'I am' of the Lord echoes the 'Here I am' of Moses. At the burning bush, God reveals his Name in the first person. He is there with Moses; he is here now as he was with Abraham, Isaac and Jacob, and as he will be with his people in the future. God names himself by saying he has been, is now and will be with his people. All tenses are present in the Name because time past and time future are all embraced in God's eternal now.

In Talmudic tradition, the repetition of 'I am' was indicative of God's pledge to Moses that he would not just save them from their present sufferings but would be with them to deliver them from sufferings and trials in the future. Later Jewish mystics were to link the repetition with God's motive in creation. The limitless God who transcends all categories

– the *En-sof* or 'God in himself' – desired to behold himself because, in the words of the *Zohar*, 'Face did not gaze on face'. The second 'I am' will reflect as in a mirror the absolute reality of the source of all being. For the Christian, the incarnational and Trinitarian aspects are readily apparent.

Later, again on Sinai, God reveals his Name for a second time. The Israelites had apostatised and worshipped the Golden Calf. After Moses had cut the second set of the tables of stone, he went up Mount Sinai and interceded for the unfaithful people, asking that he might see the glory of the Lord. We read:

> Now the Lord descended in the cloud and stood with him there, and proclaimed the name of the Lord [YHWH]. And the Lord passed before him, and proclaimed, 'The Lord, the Lord God [YHWH, YHWH ELOHIM] merciful and gracious, long-suffering, and abounding in goodness and truth'. [*Ex* 34:5–6]

The precise interpretation of the four root consonants of the Name YHWH has been a matter for intense speculation and has generated a vast and extensive literature. This Name has become known as the *Tetragrammaton* from the Greek *tettara* (four) and *gramma* (letter). As we have said, the Divine Name YHWH is connected with the verb '*hyh*' or '*hwh*', 'to be', and is in the third person singular, i.e. 'He is' or 'He who is'. Some scholars have interpreted the Name in a causative sense, as 'the one who causes to be'. The *Septuagint* gives 'I am the one who is'. God's Name defines his essence. As such, the name cannot be revealed: God both reveals and hides his Name; yet, paradoxically, God's answer to Moses will be sufficient to satisfy the questions of the Israelites when they ask who has sent him. The sense is conveyed that God will actively manifest himself to his people: 'I will be what I will be'. In the future, the eternal God will manifest his everlasting love for his people by being with them to save and redeem them.

The Name of YHWH is not a name in the usual sense of the word. Our problem in understanding the divine Name lies in the fact that normally names have the effect of making a thing an object. We use names to comprehend the world around us, to distinguish objects and set them in a framework. God can indeed be the object of our thought, but our minds cannot comprehend him nor can he be reduced to the level of an object among other objects.

The Tetragrammaton truly evokes the reality of God himself. To quote again from the *Catechism*:

> The revelation of the ineffable name 'I Am Who I Am' contains then the truth that God alone *IS*. The Greek Septuagint translation of the Hebrew Scriptures, and following it the Church's Tradition, understood the divine name in this sense: God is the fullness of Being and of every perfection, without origin and without end. All creatures receive all that they are and have from him; but he alone is his very being, and he is of himself everything that he is.[2]

The Name of the four letters – *Yod-Heh-Vav-Heh* – is the distinctive Name in the Old Testament, expressing God's eternity and his loving-kindness and mercy. It points to the Ineffable Name of God, his self-subsistent being, which God alone IS, and it is the eternal and ineffable Name of God that holds all other names in being.

---

1 *Catechism of the Catholic Church*, para. 203.
2 *Catechism of the Catholic Church*, para. 213.

# The Mystery of the Name

*O Lord God, You have begun to show Your servant Your*
*greatness and Your mighty hand, for what god is there in*
*heaven or on earth who can do anything like Your works*
*and Your mighty deeds?*   [*Deut* 3:24]

The enigmatic and mysterious nature of the Name of YHWH extends
even to the way in which it should be pronounced. Hebrew does not have
letters for vowels as such. Out of their profound reverence for the Name
of God, the Jews normally substituted the title *Adonai* (Lord) whenever
the Tetragrammaton occurred in the text. Many centuries later, the
Massoretes added vowel signs above and below the sacred consonantal
text to facilitate their pronunciation and standardise the oral tradition.
But, whenever the word 'YHWH' was written, they used the vowel
markings of the substituted title 'Adonai' as a sign that this title was to be
read in its place whenever the Name appeared in the sacred text. As
Emmanuel Levinas, the Jewish philosopher, has commented, 'The name
Adonai – which, in its turn, must not be pronounced in vain – is the name
of the Tetragrammaton. The name has a name!' [1] In fact, it was through a
Christian misunderstanding of this practice that the vowels of *Adonai*
came actually to be inserted into the consonants of 'YHWH' and the
incorrect neologism 'JeHoVaH' began to appear in some Christian
translations of the Hebrew Bible.

After the destruction of the Temple in 70 AD, in Rabbinic Judaism,
even the act of writing the sacred Name was surrounded by rituals that
reinforced the holiness of the Name. A scribe who wrote *Torah* scrolls or
the scriptural passages to be placed in *mezuzot* or in *tefillin* (phylacteries)
was required, before writing the Name, to immerse himself in the *mikveh*
(the ritual bath), a practice that had been previously required before
entering the Temple Mount. Similarly, before writing the Name of the
Lord, a scribe would first break the pen he had been using, take up a new
pen for the Holy Name, and then break that pen so that it might never be
used again to write any other word.

Writing the Name of God as such is not forbidden but, following *Deuteronomy* 12:3, the Rabbis taught that a Name of God may never be erased or defaced. Hence any Name of God may never be written casually, and extreme care is taken to avoid any possibility of the written Name being erased or defaced. Thus, when writing the number 15, which in Hebrew might be written as *Yod-Heh* (10-5) and which would thus constitute the divine Name (*Yah*), the form *Tet-Vav* (9-6) is used instead. Recently, *The Jerusalem Report* inadvertently published the Tetragrammaton inside a photograph submitted by an advertiser. A reader wrote in to say that this error could result in a reader taking the magazine into an unclean place or disposing of it in a disrespectful manner (e.g. into the rubbish bin). To avoid desecrating the holiest of names, the page or magazine should be taken to an Orthodox rabbi or placed in the *Shamos* box in a synagogue (a *shamos* or *shammash* is a sexton). The Editor of the magazine apologised for the unintended appearance of the Tetragrammaton and assured readers that it was the policy of *The Jerusalem Report* to avoid publishing the Tetragrammaton.

This reverence for the Tetragrammaton is still very much a part of the spirituality of Orthodox Jews and even of modern colloquial Hebrew. The Talmudic prohibition on pronouncing the name of God is only concerned with the four-letter Name but, outside of prayer and study, a Jew will avoid pronouncing even the other Names of God. Thus God may be referred to simply as *ha-Shem* – 'the Name' – or by some other periphrasis. Often this is done by substituting letters or syllables, and thus 'Adonai' becomes 'Adoshem', 'Elohaynu' (our God) and 'Elohim' (God) become 'Elokaynu' and 'Elokim'.

In the Greek translation of the Old Testament, the Septuagint, 'Kyrios' ('Lord') is used in place of 'YHWH,' a practice followed by most English translations. The *Catechism* comments thus on the Greek version of the divine Name as 'He Who Is':

> God is 'He Who Is,' from everlasting to everlasting, and as such remains ever faithful to himself and to his promises. The revelation of the ineffable name 'I AM WHO AM' contains then the truth that God alone IS. The Greek Septuagint translation of the Hebrew Scriptures, and following it the Church's Tradition, understood

the divine name in this sense: God is the fullness of Being and of every perfection, without origin and without end. All creatures receive all that they are and have from him; but he alone is his very being, and he is of himself everything that he is.[2]

The exact pronunciation of YHWH is no longer known with certainty. With their profound sense of the holiness of the Name and conscious of the prohibition in the Decalogue of taking the Lord's Name in vain, the Jews were reluctant to pronounce it aloud. In part, this may have its origin in a desire to put a hedge around the law against blaspheming the Name in *Leviticus* 24:11, 16: the Hebrew word for 'blaspheme' (*nachav*) can also mean 'express,' 'specify,' or 'designate'. By the third century BC, or earlier, this reluctance solidified into a legal prohibition against pronouncing the Name. In the early Rabbinic period, the distinctive Name (*Shem Ha-meforash*) was pronounced only within the Temple. Outside the Temple, in the synagogue, substitute names were employed. Even when the High Priest spoke the Name in the Temple once every year, the singing of the Levites deliberately drowned out the sound lest it be overheard.

After the Fall of the Temple, the Sages transmitted the original pronunciation to a select band of their disciples once every seventh year, but this tradition eventually ceased. By the third century AD, the explicit pronunciation of the Name was regarded as a capital offence. In fact, even in the Septuagint translation of the Old Testament dating from approximately 250 BC, there is evidence that a ban on the direct pronunciation of the Name already existed. The Septuagint translates *Leviticus* 24:16 thus:

> And whoever blasphemes the name of the Lord shall surely be put to death. All the congregation shall certainly stone him, the stranger as well as him who is born in the land. When he blasphemes the name of the Lord, he shall be put to death as 'whoever names the Name of the Lord'.

In his *Antiquities*, Josephus writes that it is unlawful to say the Name.[3] The *Talmud* forbade the saying of the Name aloud, and gradually the original pronunciation was lost.

Our familiar version *Yahweh* represents modern scholarship's best guess at recreating the original vocalisation as derived from certain texts found in the early Church Fathers, especially from a fourth-century reference by Theodoret of Cyprus, giving the Samaritan version. But, at best, *Yahweh* is an approximation only, and it is by no means proven beyond all doubt. Since the form Yahweh has become widely known, largely through the influence of the Jerusalem Bible translation, this form is used generally throughout this book, rather than the less familiar – but probably more accurate – purely consonantal form of *YHWH*.

What is certain is that the theme of the Name runs like a golden thread throughout the Old Testament. God's divine power and glory are constantly seen as present and active in his Name. The angel in whom God has set his Name leads Israel through the desert to the Promised Land. Closely related to this idea is that of the *Shekhinah*, the protective and tabernacling presence of Yahweh with his People. The word *Shekhinah* comes from the word *shakhan*, 'to dwell', and refers to the presence or indwelling of God in a certain place. Although the term is used explicitly only after the Old Testament, it describes an important motif in the Hebrew Bible, especially in the Deuteronomic writings where the *Shekhinah* is very closely linked to the theme of the Name. In later Rabbinic thought, the *Shekhinah* came to express the tenderness and compassion of God's presence with his suffering people, whether at the bedside of the sick or in mourning at the Temple Wall after the destruction of the Temple by the Romans. Tenderly God gathers his People together under the protective shelter of the wings of the *Shekhinah*. In the Targums, Aramaic versions of the Scriptures often used in the synagogues of Jesus' time for those who did not understand Hebrew, 'Name' and '*Shekhinah*' were sometimes used as synonyms. Thus the *Targum Onkelos*, which dates from the second century, translates *Deuteronomy* 12:5, 'to put his Name there', as 'to rest his *Shekhinah* there'. The Name of God expresses his Presence with mankind. Significantly, the Targums often transcribed the divine name Yahweh as 'Memra' (Word).

Although in the Old Testament, the Scripture scholars speak of a 'quasi-personification' of attributes of God such as his Wisdom and his Word, which act almost as an agent between God and his creation, there is an essential difference between these concepts and that of the Name.

Writing on the Biblical assertion that God's Name and God himself mean and are the same thing, the Lutheran scholar Ernst Lohmeyer commented:

> God's name describes him in the totality, the uniqueness, of his being and action. Whoever therefore knows God's Name stands at the door of unspeakable mysteries and light unutterable; in later words, on the threshold leading from the *Deus revelatus* to the *Deus absconditus*, from the glory of God to his holiness. So an aura of reverence and adoration surrounds the Name, and all the glory of the heavenly world, which never grows weary of praising God's Name.
>
> Among the functions exercised by the concept of the name of God, the first is that the name characterises God as person, as an immeasurable and infinite 'I'; it keeps him from floating off into the lofty heights of the 'Godhead' or from dissolving into the incomprehensible expanses of pantheism. This infinite 'I' of God demands a 'Thou', or countless 'Thou's; it acts and wills, plans and creates. So the Name of God also offers the possibility and the necessity of a world which he creates and directs, and therefore the idea of a process from creation to consummation. Only then is the problem of this name rightly seen that, in signifying God, the Name at the same time includes the idea of a world, and in presupposing this, still in so doing speaks only of God. So the Name of God denotes a threshold in an ever wider sense: it is a threshold from God's conception of the world to the creation of the world, from God's nature to his revelation, from his unity to the multiplicity of created things and beings, from his holiness to the world.[4]

This theology of the Name enabled the inspired writers to convey the idea of a 'localised' presence of the God who transcends the created order. Although Yahweh dwells in heaven, he chooses a place in which to cause his Name to dwell [*Deut* 12:11, 14:23, 16:6 and 14:24]. Dwelling in the Temple, the Name of Yahweh is the manifestation and sign of his presence with Israel, of his protection and covenant love, his *hesed*. Mount Zion is 'the place of the Name of the Lord of hosts' [*Is* 18:7].

Solomon builds the Temple as the house of the Name of Yahweh [*1 Kings* 8:14–21]. His prayer of dedication of the Temple acknowledges that the heavens cannot contain God. He entreats God that his eyes 'may be open night and day toward this house, the place of which you said, 'My name shall be there', that you may heed the prayer that your servant prays toward this place' [*1 Kings* 8:29]. The Gentiles will hear of Yahweh's great Name and come and pray towards the Temple. Then Yahweh will hear their prayer

> ... in heaven Your dwelling place, and do according to all for which the foreigner calls to you, that all peoples of the earth may know your name and fear you, as do your people Israel, and that they may know that this temple which I have built is called by your name. [*1 Kings* 8:43]

There is a growing tendency in the Old Testament to treat the Name almost as if it were a person in its own right. God's self is, as it were, concentrated and expressed in the divine Name. Isaiah looks forward to the coming of the Name, for where the Name is, there is Yahweh, approaching in majesty to save his people:

> Behold, the name of the Lord comes from afar, burning with his anger, and his burden is heavy; his lips are full of indignation, and his tongue like a devouring fire. [*Is* 30:27]

The Psalms are full of references to the Name of the Lord:

> O God, save me by your name,
> By your power, uphold my cause.
> I will sacrifice to you with willing heart
> and praise your name for it is good. [*Ps* 54:1,8]

Always the Lord is 'true to his name', and the Psalmists find in that Name their joy, their hope, their exultation, their refuge and their salvation. When the priests bless the people, they 'put' the Name on the Israelites:

> The Lord bless you and keep you; the Lord make his face shine upon you, and be gracious to you; the Lord lift up his countenance upon you, and give you peace. So they shall put My name on the children of Israel, and I will bless them. [*Num* 6:24–27]

The prophet Micah pictures the Messianic age as an eternal walking in the Name of Yahweh, and later Judaism came to see the themes of Name and Kingdom as inseparably linked. The coming of the Kingdom and the hallowing of the Name are bound together. Israel's whole mission and vocation are to walk eternally in the Name of Yahweh:

> For all people walk each in the name of his god, but we will walk in the name of the Lord our God forever and ever.   [*Mic* 4:5]

Zechariah's prophecy of the Messianic age contains a text of key importance:

> And the Lord shall be King over all the earth. In that day it shall be – 'The Lord is one', and his name one. [*Zech* 14:9]

This verse was later to be incorporated into the *Alenu* prayer for *Rosh Hashanah* (the New Year), the prayer which expresses all the heartfelt longing of Israel for the coming of the Kingdom. To this day, this prayer concludes the official services of the synagogues. The striking parallels between the *Alenu* and the early Christian hymn quoted by Paul in *Philippians* are plain to see. They show how the profoundly Jewish spirituality of the Name of Yahweh prepares the way for the spirituality of the Name of Jesus. The following quotation comes from the *Siddur*, the Jewish prayer book:

> Let all the inhabitants of the world perceive and know that unto thee every knee must bow, every tongue must swear. Before thee, O Lord our God, let them bow and fall; and unto thy glorious name let them give honour, let them all accept the yoke of thy kingdom, and do thou reign over them speedily, and for ever and ever. For the kingdom is thine, and to all eternity thou wilt reign in glory, as it is written in thy Law, The Lord shall reign for ever and ever. And it is said, And the Lord shall be king over all the earth, in that day shall the Lord be One, and his name One.[5]

Devotion to the Name of Yahweh blossomed in post-Biblical Judaism. During his time at the Hebrew University in Jerusalem between 1925 and 1965, and afterwards in his retirement, Gershom Scholem produced a series of historical studies of Jewish mysticism that demonstrated his contention that the mysticism of the Name is the characteristic quality of Jewish spirituality. The old Rabbinic adage 'His Name is He, and He is the Name' lies at the core of the Jewish faith.

In the Middle Ages, the vast esoteric system of the *Kabbalah* developed, drawing on much earlier sources. *Kabbalah* comes from the Hebrew 'k-b-l' which means 'to receive' in the sense of 'tradition'. *Kabbalah* may be best described as a highly arcane and symbolic way of thinking about God and his relationship with creation. Although it takes many divergent forms, the *Kabbalah* found its best-known and quintessential expression in the *Sepher Zohar* (the Book of Bright Splendour). Rapidly acquiring an almost canonical status, the *Zohar* was produced around the year 1290 and is generally attributed to the Spanish Kabbalist Moses de Leon, either as author or as final redactor, although he himself claimed that it was the work of the second-century rabbi, Simeon bar Yohani.

Borrowing elements from Neo-Platonism and Gnosticism, the *Zohar* is a vast *midrash* (i.e. an exposition of scriptural texts) on the inner mystical meaning of the *Torah*. Written in Aramaic, the *Zohar* is a theosophical work that sees all of the human reality depicted in the *Torah* as reflecting aspects of God himself and revealing his inner life.

Drawing on the verse of *Genesis*, 'And God said, let there be light', the Kabbalists believed that language preceded creation. Since the language used by God was Hebrew, the Kabbalists saw hidden mystical properties in the Hebrew language. In fact, they believed that behind the visible veil of the created world, the ten divine emanations or *sefirot* which express God's creative act could be known. These emanations are linked to the idea of the creative power of the letters of the Hebrew alphabet, an alphabet in which letters also serve as numbers.

The *Kabbalah* is not one single coherent system but rather a vast tradition that has many different versions and schools. Within that diverse system, the *Zohar* is the nearest that the *Kabbalah* has to what we might term a 'canonical' text. Without doubt, the *Zohar* contains much that is bizarre and exotic – such as 'gilgul,' the doctrine of the transmigration of souls – but, amidst much dross, there are many valuable insights that have had a profound influence on Judaism. For all its obscurity and inaccessibility, and in spite of modern New Age vulgarisations, the *Zohar* rightly enjoys its seminal position in the history of Jewish mysticism[6].

40

One of the most systematic presentations of the Kabbalistic doctrine of the divine Name is to be found in an obscure Zoharic text *The Secrets of the Letters of the Divine Name*, first translated into English from the Aramaic only as recently as 1988, by Stephen Wald. He writes:

> If paradox is a characteristic of truth, then we are now approaching the truth of the Divine Name, for the concept of the Divine Name is highly paradoxical. At the same time, the Divine Name, which is essentially defined as Mercy, is a simple concept, as simple and as paradoxical as human love itself ... like the human lover, the price God pays for the possibility of love is the threat of betrayal – for freedom to love God is also freedom to reject Him. 'Ultimately God's fate is in human hands: if Man chooses to love God, then God's aspirations as lover are fulfilled – Man and God are integrated into a unity of love (in which Man does not cease to be finite). If Man rejects God, then Man is separated from God, and finitude ceases to be an expression of God's goodness and infinity – the Indwelling is driven from the world.[7]

The concept of human love as a free relationship between two lovers is understood intuitively to be a higher form of perfection than the love of any solitary lover – certainly higher than any form of compelled love. Similarly, God's infinite love is incomplete so long as it does not manifest itself as real love between God and the finite world, which stands freely outside Him.[7]

For the Christian, we can see much in the *Kabbalah* that seems to cry out for the doctrine of the Trinity and of the Incarnation as the fulfilment of the *Torah*.

In their mystical writings, the Kabbalists taught that when the High Priest uttered the divine Name according to its secret pronunciation, he became a channel of divine grace between the Creator and creation. The Name of Yahweh is an inexhaustible mystery, revealing to Israel the wonder of his being which is one with his graciousness and mercy, his steadfast love and faithfulness. God's Name, his innermost being, is identified with his compassion for humanity and his desire to come close to them. Thus the Name of God acts as a bridge between the transcendent God and the universe he has made.

Rabbinic thought came to associate the name of Yahweh with God's special relationship with his People Israel, in contrast with the more generic name of *Elohim* which denotes God in his universal aspect. The Jewish mystics taught that the Name Yahweh represented the divine *Rahamim,* the compassion of God, which mediates between his *Hesed*, his merciful love, and his *Gevurah* or *Din*, his stern justice. God gives life to the whole world through the Tetragrammaton. The divine *Rahamim* is linked to the feast of *Sukkot*, the festival that celebrates the gathering-in of the harvest, and looks forward in time to the last days when all nations will serve God as one.

We should never forget that nothing happens by chance in God's dealings with mankind or in the words and names that he uses in revelation. All is a unity, and the purpose behind those dealings is God's tender mercy. This applies to the use of the divine names in the Old Testament. As an illustration of this, and of the link between the revelation of the Name and God's compassion, we can cite a *Midrash* on why the Lord spoke to Moses out of a burning thorn bush:

> And God called unto him out of the midst of the bush [*Ex* 3:4].
> The Holy One said to Moses: Do you not sense that I live in distress whenever Israel find themselves in distress? Just look at the place out of which I speak to you – out of a thorn bush. I – if one dare attribute such words to God – fully share in their distress, as implied in the words 'In all their affliction, he is afflicted' [*Is* 63:9].[8]

For the very first time, God calls Israel 'my people'. We see the divine mercy and tenderness in the revelation of the Name. The medieval Jewish commentator Rashi noted that the vision was in the very heart [Hebrew *lev*] of the burning bush.

The divine compassion is shown by the choice of a thorn bush, the wild acacia, and not another tree. God suffers with Israel and hence appears in the lowliest plant.

The Name revealed to Moses from the heart of the burning thorn bush is the Name of the One who will hang on the Cross crowned with thorns. The promise to Moses had been that Yahweh would be with his People. Jesus is Yahweh with us. Yahweh-with-us is Jesus. In Christian iconography, the nimbus that surrounds the head of Christ is normally inscribed with the three Greek letters 'ο ωΝ', 'He who is'. In Jesus, that promise made to Moses is fulfilled for all ages and for all men.

In the old dispensation, the New Testament is concealed and, in the new dispensation, it is revealed. The Old Testament devotion to the Name of Yahweh prepared the way for devotion to the Name of Jesus. Before the establishment of the kingdom of Israel, Manoah asked the name of the angel of the Lord. The angel replied with a question: 'Why do you ask my name? It is too wonderful' [*Judg* 13:18]. The Name of Yahweh, the Tetragrammaton, lies beyond man's understanding and yet it is the revelation of God, of his merciful Presence. Israel's religious quest is to behold the face of the Lord and to hear his Name. When the time had been fully prepared, God was to reveal his face and manifest his Name in the most wonderful way of all, by the Incarnation. Then, unasked, the angel would reveal the Name by which alone we can be saved.

---

1 E Levinas, *Beyond the Verse: Talmudic Readings and Lectures*, Indiana, 1994; p. 121. This book contains a profound essay on the Name of God.

2 *Catechism of the Catholic Church*, para. 212–3.

3 *Antiquities*, 2:12:4.

4 E Lohmeyer, *The Lord's Prayer*, London, 1965; pp. 75–6.

5 *The Authorised Daily Prayer Book of the United Hebrew Congregations of the British Commonwealth of Nations*, with a new translation by the late Rev S Singer, London, 1962; pp. 80–1.

6 The *Kabbalah* uses an extraordinarily rich poetic language of imagery and symbolism in speaking about God and his relationship with the world. This language is very easily misunderstood both by those who seek to understand it as if it were a systematic theology, and also by those are wrongly attracted by what they see as the occult nature of the *Kabbalah*. Of those who are attracted by the thought of a secret gnosis knowledge known only to an elite, the words of St Paul apply: 'Knowledge puffs up, but love edifies. And if anyone thinks that he knows anything, he knows nothing as yet as he ought to know. But if anyone loves God, this one is known by him' [*1 Cor* 8:1–3]. A very balanced note is struck by Alan Unterman: 'Although the images which the *Kabbalah* uses are very concrete and totally anthropomorphic, and may sometimes shock the sensibilities of the unwary, they are not to be taken as anything but symbolic forms conveying understanding beyond the standard conceptual levels of logical thought. The overriding emphasis within

Judaism on the individual unity of God underlies the whole Kabbalistic theosophy and indeed it very much allows the mystic so much freedom for symbolic description. It cannot be denied than non-kabbalists have misinterpreted the variety of the symbolic language, and the richness of its forms, finding it to be teaching a threefold or tenfold nature of the divine. But no kabbalist himself, however distinct his imagery may seem, ever misunderstood the symbol for the unitary reality behind it. Indeed, it was the obvious danger of misunderstanding, of the unification of symbol and reality and the resultant heresies, which kept the *Kabbalah* at the level of the esoteric. We find warnings in quite early sources against the public teaching of the mystical tradition and even against the private teaching of it to those who are unable to assimilate its symbolic nature. It was the danger of misunderstanding which helped to keep the kabbalistic tradition an oral tradition, and the opposition to writing down and publishing mystical teachings that exist into the present day.' *The Wisdom of the Jewish Mystics*, London, 1976; pp.19–20. This anthology of religious texts contains an excellent brief introduction to the Jewish mystical tradition for the general reader.

7  Stephen G Wald, *The Doctrine of the Divine Name: An Introduction to Classical Kabbalistic Theology*, Atlanta, Georgia, 1988; pp. 49–51.

8  *The Soncino Midrash Rabbah* (CD-ROM), Davka Corporation, NY, 1992–1995.

# The Giving of the Name

*We give thanks to You, O God, we give thanks!*
*For Your wondrous works declare that*
*Your name is near.* [*Ps* 7:1 (NJV)]

The light of the Name of Jesus shines forth from the very first page of the Gospels. With its profoundly Jewish background, St Matthew's Gospel opens with a genealogy that traces the origin, the 'genesis', of the Messiah back to Abraham, 'the father of Isaac, the father of Jacob.' The Messiah's lineage goes back to Abraham, the father of all Jews, with whom God had made the covenant of circumcision. Matthew's reference to the Patriarchs recalls the first revelation of the Name of Yahweh at the burning bush where God revealed himself as the God of Abraham, Isaac and Jacob.

Schematic and selective in its approach, Matthew's genealogy also demonstrates the Davidic origin of the Messiah through Joseph his adoptive father. Although Joseph is not the biological father of the Messiah, Matthew establishes the legal paternity of Joseph according to Jewish law. Normally, a Jewish father would choose the name of his son according to family tradition and custom, but here the angel tells Joseph what the name of the Virgin's son is to be. The naming of the Messiah is a sign of the divine paternity. Since the role of an angel is to bring a message from God, it is God alone who chooses the Name of the Messiah and of his Son. What is eternal begins to exist in time, and the Name of the Word-made-flesh, eternally pre-existent in the mind of God, is now made known on earth.

There is no burning bush or theophany, and the angel speaks to Joseph in a dream in the most matter-of-fact manner, telling him not to be afraid:

> Joseph, son of David, do not be afraid to take to you Mary your wife, for that which is conceived in her is of the Holy Spirit. And she will bring forth a Son, and you shall call his name Jesus, for he will save his people from their sins. [*Matt* 1:20–21]

Reassuring Joseph, the angel tells him that the child is conceived of the Holy Spirit as a result of direct divine intervention. He commands Joseph to name the child 'Jesus,' the Name which both expresses who the child is and what his mission is to be.

There are all sorts of rich Biblical echoes here. Like his father Jacob before him, Joseph had to discover that God was in this place though he knew it not. God is at work in Mary. She is indeed the gate of heaven, for in her womb she carries the Son of the Most High. She is truly *Beth-el*, the house of God. Just as the bush was aflame with the divine glory and was not consumed, so Mary carries the Word in her womb while remaining ever a virgin. As the bush was not consumed, so Mary bears the Son of God without being consumed. Just as his namesake went down to Egypt, so Joseph takes the Holy Family down to exile in Egypt. This is to fulfil what was written, that God would call his Son out of Egypt.

Our Lord is the new Israel. In *Exodus* 4:22, Israel is called God's 'first-born son', and the first revelation of the Name on the eve of the Exodus finds an unconscious echo in the revelation of the Name of Jesus. The name the people will call Jesus is 'Immanuel,' which means 'God with us'. For all time, God will be with his People. The logic of this is simple and mind-shattering: Jesus is God with us. The Name of Jesus is one with the Name of Yahweh.

In both *Matthew* and *Luke*, it is the archangel Gabriel who reveals the Name. In the book of *Daniel*, Gabriel is sent to give Daniel 'wisdom and understanding' of the vision he had been granted for Daniel is 'greatly beloved'. This is echoed in Gabriel's words to Mary, which also recall those in *Zechariah* 9:9

> Rejoice greatly, O daughter of Zion! Shout, O daughter of Jerusalem! Behold, your King is coming to you; he is just and having salvation, lowly and riding on a donkey, a colt, the foal of a donkey.

We find in Mary's great song of praise the same exultant note of joy of the Psalmist: 'Rejoice in the Lord, O you righteous, and give thanks to his holy name!' The Lord, Yahweh, is with Mary. She is the dwelling-place of the Name, the new Ark of the Covenant.

Much perplexed by the angel's words, Mary wonders what kind of greeting this might be, only to be told: 'And behold, you will conceive in your womb and bring forth a Son, and shall call his name Jesus' [*Lk* 1:31].

Gabriel tells her that 'The Holy Spirit will come upon you, and the power of the Most High will overshadow you; therefore, also, that Holy One who is to be born will be called the Son of God'. [*Lk* 1:35]

The *Shekhinah* had been present in the burning bush and is now present in the Blessed Virgin. In Rabbinic tradition, the cloud of the Tabernacle in *Exodus* 40:34–38 was the cloud of the *Shekhinah*. Mary is 'overshadowed' by the Holy Spirit and becomes the place of the *Shekhinah*, the New Ark of the Covenant, the dwelling place for the Name:

> For the cloud of the Lord was above the tabernacle by day, and fire was over it by night, in the sight of all the house of Israel, throughout all their journeys. [*Ex* 40:38]

In her song, she praises the Name of the Lord for 'the Mighty One has done great things for me, and holy is his name'.

After eight days had passed from the birth of the Messiah, the time came to circumcise the child. Obedient to God's word, Mary and Joseph call him Jesus, the name given by the angel before he was conceived in the womb. He becomes a child of the covenant and henceforth bears this Name which sums up all he is and all he will do. There is nothing arbitrary here; nothing is left to chance. Before the moment when the Incarnation takes place in time, Gabriel reveals to Mary the Name that from all eternity has existed in the mind of God, the name of God with us, and God with us is Jesus. The prophecy of Isaiah is fulfilled:

> The Gentiles shall see your righteousness, and all kings your glory. You shall be called by a new name, which the mouth of the Lord will name. [*Is* 62:2]

The name is new because the Word is made flesh and henceforth all mankind shall see the light of his glory.

The mission of an angel is to bring a message from God, and Gabriel's message is the Good News of Jesus. This is the Good News that must be proclaimed to the whole of creation, to a creation which was made for the glory of the Name and groans in travail as it awaits redemption after Adam's sin.

With the coming of the Messiah, the promise of the divine mercy contained in the revelation of the divine mercy in the Name of Yahweh finds its fulfilment. In his book *On the Art of the Kabbalah*, the sixteenth-century Christian Kabbalist, Johann Reuchlin, put the following words into the mouth of the angel Raziel who is sent to console the grief-stricken Adam:

> Don't lie there shuddering, burdened with grief, thinking of your responsibility for bringing the race of man to perdition. The primal sin will be purged in this way: from your seed will be born a just man, a man of peace, a hero whose name will in pity contain these four letters – Yahweh – and through his upright trustfulness and peaceable sacrifice will put out his hand, and take from the Tree of Life, and the fruit of that Tree will be salvation to all who hope for it.[1]

The shining splendour of the Name of Jesus will dispel all darkness. In its radiant brilliance, all shall be well and all manner of thing shall be well. The King has come into his own and the long exile of the world is over, for the time of restoration has begun. God's Name is One, but from now on it can never be the name of a stranger, beyond the lips of man or known only to a select group of initiates. The Name is on our lips, in our mind and in our heart. If we confess with our mouth that Jesus is Lord and believe in our heart that God raised Him from the dead, we shall be saved.

---

1  J Reuchlin, *On the Art of the Kabbalah: De Arte Cabalistica*, trans. M & S Goodman, Lincoln (Nebraska) and London, 1993; p.73.

# Yahweh and Yeshua

*On the eighth day, when it was time for his brit-milah,*
*he was given the name Yeshua, which is what the angel*
*called him before his conception.*   [*Lk* 2:21 (JNT)[1]]

In Jesus, the Name takes flesh and salvation comes among us. As we have seen, the primary Biblical emphasis is not so much on God's essence but on his actions, on the qualities of his being radiating out to man. The Word is the true light that shines in the dark and enlightens all men, the light that has come into our world. We see the radiance of this light at the time of Paul's conversion. On the road to Damascus, the light of the *Shekhinah* shone round Saul and he fell to the ground. He heard a voice say to him: 'Saul, Saul, why do you persecute me?' In fear and trembling like Moses before him, Saul asks 'Who are you, Lord?' and the voice, speaking in Hebrew, reveals his Name: 'I am Jesus, whom you are persecuting'. The Lord makes himself known by this Name. The very heart of Paul's preaching is that Jesus is Lord.

Since God's own Name is one with what he is, it transcends totally our ability to understand or comprehend it. It is the very intensity of the divine light that hides Him in darkness. But that is not the end of the story. Out of love for his creation, God reaches out to us in his actions, in the divine energies in which he is truly present. The divine energies span the gulf between the Creator and creature, for the divine light shines forth from the darkness. The Lord, who holds creation in the palm of his hand, tells us his Name. His Name reveals that he is and will be with us, the Saviour, the compassionate One, the One who was, who is and will be, Yahweh.

God's love for his People stops at nothing. His gift to us is himself and his love has no limits or boundaries. The Father sends his Son who makes known to us all the mysteries contained in his Name, the infinite compassion in his heart for man. Speaking of the Cross, when men shall gaze on the One whom they have pierced, Christ says 'When you have lifted up the Son of man, then you will know that I Am He' [*Jn* 8:28]. When Philip asked to see the Father, Our Lord answered by saying that to have seen him was to have seen the Father. So it is with the Name of Yahweh. To know Jesus is to know He who is.

In the New Covenant, the continuation and fulfilment of the Old, the Pentagrammaton, the five letter name is revealed – the Name of Jesus, which in Hebrew and Aramaic is 'Yeshua'. Now, the Name can be pronounced. The five sacred letters of the Name can be vocalised. Just as the Word is made flesh and becomes visible, so too the Name can now not only be uttered, but can be invoked by all, for in Jesus dwells all the fullness of the divinity. His is the Name which is above all other names.[2]

The New Testament makes an inseparable link between the Name, Person and work of God, and the Name, Person and work of Jesus. The Name of Jesus is the integral, authorised manifestation of all the mysteries contained in the Name of God, the ineffable Name, subsistent and identical with the divine essence. Applied to the Messiah, the name 'Jesus' expresses both the humanity and the divine mission of the Incarnate Word, Immanuel, God with us.

Whenever God gives a name to a man or a woman in Scripture, that name expresses their mission and their being. The Greek *Iesous* represents the Hebrew and Aramaic 'Yeshua', and is usually translated as 'Yahweh saves' or 'Yahweh is salvation'. The Hebrew for 'He will save' is *yoshia*, and comes from the same root as *Yeshua*. Although this name as such is not unique to Jesus, being a late contracted form of 'Joshua' [*Yehoshuah*], it is strictly speaking proper only to Mary's son because 'He will save his people from their sins'. He alone is the true Jesus. In other words, the very Name of Jesus declares his mission: Jesus comes to us in order to be our Jesus.

The Scriptures give us a definition of the name of Joshua from which the Name of Yeshua comes:

> A valiant leader was Joshua, son of Nun, assistant to Moses in the prophetic office, formed to be, as his name implies, the great saviour of God's chosen ones, to punish the enemy and to win the inheritance for Israel. [*Sir* 46:1]

Moses gave the name Joshua (Yahweh saves) to Hoshea (saviour or deliverer), to stress that it would be the Lord himself who would save his people. Joshua himself is not the saviour: it is the Lord himself who alone can save his people. His name is not absolute but provisional, pointing to the true Joshua. Jesus receives the Name of Jesus because he will save the people from their sins. What is foreshadowed in Joshua is fulfilled in a transcendent manner in Jesus who is the Saviour, the one who overcomes Satan and wins an eternal inheritance for God's People. Jesus does not lead Israel across a physical river into a physical land. By being baptised by John in the river Jordan, Christ sanctifies the whole of creation. By his death and resurrection, He leads us through the waters of baptism into the Promised Land to share in the very life of God himself.

Nothing is left to chance. It is highly significant that the Archangel Gabriel revealed the Name of Jesus to Mary before the conception of the child, and that it is the Name of Jesus that the angels use at the Ascension. In Rabbinic thought, the Name of the Messiah is one of the things that existed before the creation of the cosmos: his coming is a part of God's original design, programmed into the very act of creation itself.

The Name of Jesus pre-existed in God from all eternity. As Father, God knows the Son and the Name of the Incarnate Word. Thus the Name of Jesus is an eternal mystery, revealing the mystery of the Incarnate Word. Our Lord's Name should never be seen as a mere external or accidental signification of the Word, for the Word himself is truly our saviour, uniting in his own divine Person the two natures, human and divine. The Name of Jesus expresses the totality of the Word made flesh.

The same God of the Patriarchs who revealed himself to Moses as 'I am' is now to be with his people for ever by taking our human nature to himself. The Sacred Humanity is 'bone of our bone, and flesh of our flesh'. Yahweh is with his People in the most intimate way of all: the heavens are rent open and God has come down among us. Hence the Name of Our Lord is not a name which simply reminds us of the saving mercy or attributes of God. It is the name of the one who is the saving mercy of God, for God alone can forgive sin. In Jesus, the Name and his divine mission are one, for the Name expresses who the Son is and what he does. The ineffable Name of Yahweh is made visible in Jesus and the Name that could not be uttered can now be invoked by all. Just as man longs to see God, so he longs to know his Name. Jesus makes known the Name of the Father, for to have seen him is to have seen the Father. As Saint Maximus the Confessor wrote in his commentary on the Lord's

Prayer: 'the name of God the Father, in its eternal subsistence, is the only begotten Son'.

Man's response to God's Word is faith, faith in the mystery of the Incarnation and Redemption. When the Christian calls on the Name of Jesus with faith, the invocation is an entering into the mystery of the Pasch of Christ, because we could not call him unless he first called us. The mystery of Jesus is made present. Our hearts are opened to the rays of love radiating from his Sacred Heart.

With this in mind, we begin to realise something of the force of texts such as the following:

> And in that day you will ask Me nothing. Most assuredly, I say to you, whatever you ask the Father in my name he will give you. [*Jn* 6:23]

> Nor is there salvation in any other, for there is no other name under heaven given among men by which we must be saved. [*Acts* 4:12]

We have already discussed the hymn in *Philippians* 2 where Our Lord receives the Name which is 'above all other names' and, as we shall see, it is in St John's Gospel that the link between the two Names is most clearly drawn. The divinity of Yeshua is shown by his use of the Name of Yahweh of himself.

Already, we can see Jesus is the Alpha and the Omega of all creation. It is not by accident that the Name of Jesus should be both the first and the last name to appear in the New Testament. Matthew's Gospel begins with the origins of 'Jesus Christ, the son of David, the son of Abraham' and the Apocalypse ends with the fervent prayer that Jesus may come and for his grace to be with all the saints. Symbolically, the Name of Jesus contains and frames the whole of the Good News of the Kingdom of God.

In that Name above all names, the promises of the old covenant and the mysteries of the new covenant find their fulfilment. St Bernardine of Siena expressed it beautifully when he wrote of the power of the Name that announces salvation to all:

> The name of Jesus is the splendour of preachers, because it causes his word to be proclaimed and heard with glowing splendour.

Whence do you think came the great, sudden and shining light of faith that filled the world, if not from the preaching of Jesus? Was it not by the light and sweetness of this name that God called us into his wonderful light? It is to us, on whom the light has shone, and who in that light see light, that the apostle addresses these apt words: 'Once you were darkness, but now you are light in the Lord; walk as sons of the light.'[3]

---

1  David H Stern, *Jewish New Testament: a translation of the New Testament that expresses its Jewishness*, Jerusalem, 1989; p.26. This is a Messianic Jewish translation of the New Testament.

2  In sixteenth-century Spain, many Christian writers were either consciously or unconsciously influenced by the thought and imagery of the *Kabbalah*. Perhaps the most notable of these was Luis de Leon (1527–1591) whose book *The Names of Christ* is one of the great masterpieces of the golden age of Spanish literature. Partially of Jewish descent on his mother's side, he was very much influenced by the *Kabbalah* and wrote thus on the relationship between the Tetragrammaton and the name of Our Lord in Hebrew: 'One aspect seems important to me. The Hebrew word for Jesus is 'Yehoshuah'. ... And in it we finds all the letters that go into the name of God in Hebrew, the so-called 'four-letter name of God' or 'Tetragrammaton,' plus two letters more. As you know, the name of God with four letters is a name that cannot be uttered, because vowels are not pronounced, because we do not know what their real sound should be, or because of the respect due to God, or else, as I have suspected sometimes, because it is like the mumbling sounds that a dumb person utters as an expression of friendship, affection, love: without a clear pattern, shapeless, as if God wanted us men to use a word to express his infinite being, a clumsy word or a sound that would make us understand that God is too large to be embraced or expressed in any clear way by our understanding and our tongue. Pronouncing such a name is tantamount to admitting that we are limited and dumb when we come face to face with God. Our confusion and our mumbling are a hymn of praise, as David declared; the name of God is ineffable and unutterable. And yet in Jesus' name two letters have been added and the name can indeed be pronounced and said out loud with a clear meaning. What happened with Christ also happened with Christ's name: It is the clear portrait of God. In Christ we see God joined to a man's soul and body. God's name, which could not be said, now has two more letters and it can be said, mysteries can be revealed, made visible, can be talked about. Christ is Jesus, that is to say, a combination of God and man, of a name that cannot be uttered and a name that can'. Luis de Leon, *The Names of Christ*: translation and introduction by Manuel Duran and William Kluback. Ramsey, New Jersey, 1984; p. 349.

3  St Bernardine of Siena, *Sermon 49, On the Name of Jesus*, quoted in *The Divine Office: The Liturgy of the Hours According to the Roman Rite*, London, 1974; Vol. 3, p. 8*.

# The Words of the Lord on His Name
# in the Synoptic Gospels

*Those who know your name will trust you; you will never*
*forsake those who seek you.* [*Ps* 9:10]

What Our Lord himself says about his Name must lie at the very heart of
our meditation on the mystery of the Name. Christ speaks to us in the
whole of Scripture, but there is a particular intensity in his own words as
recorded by the Evangelists. In the Gospels, in the most wonderful and
sublime fashion, the Word addresses each one of us directly; and it is in
the Gospels that we shall find the essence of the prayer of the Name.

We shall now look at the words of Our Lord regarding his Name as we
find them in the first three Gospels, the 'Synoptic' Gospels, so called
because they share a common viewpoint and approach. It is immediately
apparent that Christ sees the concepts of 'name,' 'person' and 'self' as
inextricably linked. The Messiah speaks of his Name in terms of its being
charged with his presence and power. It is the symbol of who and what he
is. As we have already seen, in Semitic thought 'name', 'person' and 'self'
are almost interchangeable concepts: the name is the person manifest and
expressed. Indeed, it would have been surprising if Our Lord as a Jew had
thought otherwise.

When we collate Our Lord's references to his Name in the Synoptic
Gospels, certain key themes emerge. These reflect common Semitic usage
whereby the name is used as a way of referring to actions done in his
person, on his behalf or by his authority. Thus in his Name prophecies are
made, demons exorcised and mighty deeds worked. His Name will be
used fraudulently by false Messiahs claiming his authority. To receive a
child in his Name is to receive him. The disciple will be hated because of
his Name. In his Name, the Gentiles will hope and repentance will be
preached to all the nations. Those who give up everything for the sake of
the Name will inherit eternal life. The Messiah comes 'in the name of the
Lord', and the Messianic cry of the people *Hosanna* (save us) is addressed
to him whose very name means salvation. From what Our Lord says of

his own Name, it is clear that it has a transcendent power and dignity.

One saying in particular has often been quoted, and clearly has a mystical dimension: 'where two or three are gathered in my Name, I am in the midst of them' [*Mt* 18:20]. The full import of the saying becomes evident if we compare it to the following passage from the *Talmud*:

> If two sit together and words of *Torah* pass between them, the *Shekhinah* abides between them, as it is said, 'Those who feared Adonai spoke together, and Adonai paid heed and listened, and a record was written before him for those who feared Adonai and thought on his name'. [*Avot* 3:2]

Traditionally, these words have been seen in a liturgical context, but there is a broader meaning here. Our Lord is speaking of himself as the *Shekhinah*, the immanent presence of God himself, and it may be that there is a further added dimension. The Law prescribed a quorum of ten adult Jewish males to constitute the *minyan* necessary for worship. The Christian *minyan* can consist of just two gathered in his Name. The disciples would have been aware of all these associations, and the calm statement of their Master would have startled them. Indeed, it should make us think. By gathering in the Lord's Name, we have already entered into the Holy of Holies.

When Our Lord responded to the disciples' request to teach them how to pray, he gave them a prayer that is the perfect epitome of all of the spirituality of the Old Testament and of the synagogue. The 'Our Father' rings with all sorts of rich echoes from the Jewish prayers of the day. The petition 'Hallowed be thy name' does not refer directly to the Name of Jesus, but it is obviously of great importance in any reflection on the Holy Name.

The opening invocation of the Father in heaven recalls the prayer *Avinu sh'ba Shammayim*, which begins with the words 'Our Father who art in heaven, deal with us lovingly for thy great Name's sake'. Strictly speaking, the second petition 'Hallowed be thy name' presents us with an apparent contradiction. How can man 'hallow' the Name of God since the Name of God is already infinitely holy and the source of all holiness in all creation?

We can add nothing to God's greatness, for God has no need of man's praise; but 'our desire to thank you is itself your gift. Our prayer of thanksgiving adds nothing to your greatness, but makes us grow in your grace, through Jesus Christ our Lord' (Weekday Preface IV of the Roman Missal). The Name is hallowed by our praise and adoration, and by our submission to God's will so that his glory may be revealed to all.

The primary thrust of the petition is, however, that God may hallow his own Name and manifest his glory by his mighty power. The *Catechism* draws our attention to the fact that the petition as taught by Christ is in the optative, the verbal mood used to express a desire or a wish. It is a prayer that God's will may be done by and in us. The petition corresponds to the prophecy of Ezekiel:

> Therefore say to the house of Israel, 'Thus says the Lord God: "I do not do this for your sake, O house of Israel, but for my holy name's sake, which you have profaned among the nations wherever you went. And I will sanctify my great name, which has been profaned among the nations, which you have profaned in their midst; and the nations shall know that I am the Lord", says the Lord God, "when I am hallowed in you before their eyes. For I will take you from among the nations, gather you out of all countries, and bring you into your own land. Then I will sprinkle clean water on you, and you shall be clean; I will cleanse you from all your filthiness and from all your idols. I will give you a new heart and put a new spirit within you; I will take the heart of stone out of your flesh and give you a heart of flesh." '
> [*Ezek* 36:22–6]

The same theme is found in the *Kaddish*, one of the best known of all Jewish prayers and one that goes back to the time of Christ. Although now popularly associated with mourning, the *Kaddish* is fundamentally a prayer that God may declare the holiness of his Name. It expresses all the hope and the longing of Israel for comfort and restoration:

> Magnified and sanctified be God's great name in the world which he created according to his will. May he establish his kingdom during our lifetime and during the lifetime of Israel. Let us say, Amen.
>
> May God's great name be blessed forever and ever.
>
> Blessed, glorified, honoured and extolled, adored and acclaimed be the name of the Holy One, though God is beyond all praises

and songs of adoration which can be uttered. Let us say, Amen.

May there be peace and life for all of us and for all Israel. Let us say, Amen.

Let he who makes peace in the heavens, grant peace to all of us and to all Israel. Let us say, Amen.

The Name and the Kingdom can never be separated, for the coming of the Kingdom flows naturally from the sanctification of the Name. God reveals his Name by his mighty works of salvation. To pray for the hallowing of the Name is ultimately to pray for the coming of Christ himself: 'marana tha' – 'Come, Lord Jesus'.

As well as the echo of the *Kaddish*, the petition has a possible allusion to the daily prayer of the synagogue. Known as the *Amidah* Prayer because it is said standing, the Eighteen Benedictions are said three times a day. At the end of the third paragraph, the reader responds with the *Kedushah* ('Holiness') prayer which is a sanctification of God's name and unites the liturgy of heaven and earth:

> We will sanctify thy name in the world even as they sanctify it in the highest heavens, even as they sanctify it in the highest heavens, as it is written by the hand of thy prophet: 'And they called one unto the other and said, "Holy, Holy, Holy is the Lord of hosts, the whole earth is full of his glory" '. [*Is* 6:3][1]

The idea of the sanctification of the Name ('*Kiddush ha-Shem*') is a fundamental one in Jewish thought. *Kiddush ha-Shem* reaches its highest form in martyrdom, the supreme act of witness where death is accepted rather than deny God. But *Kiddush ha-Shem* has a much wider frame of reference than the willingness to lay down one's life for the Name. It applies to any deed or action, including prayer, that bears public witness to the holiness of God and thus makes the holiness of the Name manifest in daily human life. Any good deed that increases the honour and respect given to God sanctifies his Name. Conversely, any evil deed that takes away the honour and respect that is due to God is *Chillul Ha-Shem*, the profanation of the Name.

Since ultimately it is only God who can sanctify his own Name, it is Christ himself as both God and man who is the perfect sanctifier of the

Name. Unlike fallen man, Christ as the Servant of the Lord lives a life of perfect surrender to the will of his Father: he 'trusts in the name of the Lord' [*Is* 50:10], and even in the womb of his mother Yahweh gave him his Name [*ibid.* 49:1]. Nailed to the Cross, crowned with thorns, in thirst and in agony, Christ is the perfect sanctifier of the Name. He is the true and eternal High Priest, the *cohen gadol*, offering the atoning sacrifice that ushers in the Kingdom that shall have no end.

In the Temple on the Day of Atonement, Yom Kippur, the High Priest, having first pronounced the Name of the Lord over the bullock and the scapegoat, sacrificed the bullock that was to be the sin-offering and then entered beyond the veil of the Holy of Holies for the offering of the incense. Having incensed the most holy sanctuary, he emerged from the sanctuary, slew the goat that was for the Lord and re-entered the Holy of Holies two further times to sprinkle the Holy of Holies with the blood of the bullock and the goat.

The *Letter to the Hebrews* shows how this was a symbol of what was to come:

> But we see Jesus, who was made a little lower than the angels, for the suffering of death crowned with glory and honour, that he, by the grace of God, might taste death for everyone. For it was fitting for him, for whom are all things and by whom are all things, in bringing many sons to glory, to make the captain of their salvation perfect through sufferings. For both he who sanctifies and those who are being sanctified are all of one, for which reason he is not ashamed to call them brethren, saying: 'I will declare your name to my brethren; in the midst of the assembly I will sing praise to you'. And again, 'I will put my trust in him'. Also: 'Here am I and the children whom God has given me'. [*Heb* 2:9–13]

> ... Christ came as High Priest of the good things to come, with the greater and more perfect tabernacle not made with hands, that is, not of this creation. Not with the blood of goats and calves, but with his own blood he entered the Most Holy Place once for all, having obtained eternal redemption. [*Heb* 9:11–12]

As Cardinal Ratzinger has profoundly observed, the blood of Jesus calls all to reconciliation. It has become, as the *Letter to the Hebrews* shows, itself 'a permanent Day of Atonement of God' [2]. Eternally, Christ hallows the Name before us and on our behalf.

Our Lord's great cry on the Cross – *'Eloi, Eloi, lama sabach-thani?'* – is answered in the very Psalm from which he quotes: the Servant of the Lord is forsaken in order that he may come to 'tell of Your name to my brethren' [*Ps* 21]. The Suffering Servant is despised and rejected by men, a man of sorrows and acquainted with grief, upon whom was laid the chastisement that makes us whole.

Again, the Psalms foretell that the one who sanctifies the Name will be raised on high:

> Whoever clings to me I will deliver;
> Whoever knows my name I will set on high.
> All who call upon me I will answer;
> I will be with them in distress;
> I will deliver them and give them honour.
> [*Ps* 91:14–15 (NJV)]

Thus the paschal mystery of Christ is the supreme, unique and all-embracing act of *Kiddush ha-Shem,* the perfect hallowing of the Name, by which God manifests the holiness of his Name before the nations. The Orthodox writer, Olivier Clément, stated it succinctly when he observed: 'For the Son is the Father's eternal Name, which he hallowed to the point of death on the cross'. This is the ultimate act of redemptive and suffering love, and thus the cross becomes the new Jacob's ladder between heaven and earth. Since man is called to hallow the Name of God and yet is caught in the world of sin and death, powerless and enslaved, only the second Adam can truly hallow the Name because he is both God and man. The cross vindicates the justice and mercy of God for all who see it with the eyes of faith, Jew and Gentile alike:

> All the earth shall remember and return to the Lord,
> all the families of the nations will worship before Him
> for the kingdom is the Lord's; he is ruler of the nations.
> [*Ps* 21:28–9]

The kingly power that reconciles God and man is not of this world: it shines forth at the very moment when darkness covers the whole land and the sun is obscured. Luke tells how one of the criminals crucified with Christ derided Him: 'if you are the Christ, save yourself and us'. But the other criminal was transformed by grace. We see the kingly power dramatically at work in the change of heart of the repentant thief. Transformed and enlightened by grace, he saw that Jesus was the Messiah and asked for salvation: 'Jesus, remember me when you come into your kingdom'. Probably without realising the full import of his words, the penitent thief called on the Name of the Lord and received salvation, the promise that he will be with the Messiah that day in Paradise. Jesus was for him a Jesus.

As he died on the Cross, Christ commended himself to his Father and breathed forth his spirit. The veil of the Temple was rent in two and, on guard at the foot of the cross, the Roman centurion, the representative of the nations, witnessed the death of Christ. Profoundly moved by all that he had seen and heard but, like the penitent thief, probably unaware of the full significance of his own words, the Gentile soldier declared that Christ was the son of God. Here we already have in seed what the Church will become, for the dividing wall between Jew and Gentile has been torn down.

It is perhaps fitting to close this chapter with further words taken from the *Kaddish*, words that in a later period were to become especially associated with mourning, but which remain always, above all, a paean of praise for the Holy Name:

> Blessed, praised and glorified, exalted, extolled and honoured, magnified and lauded be the name of the Holy One, blessed be he; though he be high above all the blessings and hymns, praises and consolations, which are uttered in the world; and say ye, Amen.

> Let the name of the Lord be blessed from this time forth and for evermore...

---

1 The heavenly *Kedushah* is described in a Jewish apocalypse dating from the fifth to sixth century AD: 'Rivers of joy, rivers of rejoicing, rivers of gladness, rivers of exultation,

rivers of love, rivers of friendship pour out from the throne of glory, and, gathering strength, flow through the gates of the paths of the heaven of Arabot, at the melodious sound of his creatures' harps, at the exultant sound of the drums of his wheels, at the sound of the cymbal music of his cherubim. The sound swells and bursts out in a mighty rush – Holy, holy, holy, Lord of hosts, the whole earth is full of glory' [Appendix to *3 Enoch* 22B, 7]. Translated by P Alexander in *The Old Testament Pseudipigrapha: Vol. 1, Apocalyptic literature and testaments*, J H Charlesworth (ed.), London, 1983.

2  In an address given at the International Jewish-Christian Conference in Jerusalem to mark the promulgation of the new *Catechism*. Cardinal Ratzinger has continually stressed the Jewishness of Christianity and the importance of ongoing links between Christianity and Judaism.

# 'Before Abraham came into being, I Am':
# The Name in St John's Gospel

*I, even I, am He who comforts you.*   [*Is* 51:12a]

Speaking at a General Audience held on 26th November 1996, Pope John Paul II gave a catechesis on how Jesus made the divine Name his own. We can take his words as our starting point as we explore the theme of the Name in the Gospel of the Beloved Disciple.

The Pope began his address by noting that in the opening words of St John's Gospel – 'In the beginning was the Word' – St John is focusing our attention not on the circumstances of Christ's human birth, but on the mystery of his divine pre-existence. St John is speaking of the absolute beginning, 'the beginning without beginning', eternity itself. The Johannine 'in the beginning' echoes the 'in the beginning' of Genesis. In Genesis, the reference is to the beginning of time, but in John, when the Word is mentioned, the reference is to eternity.

Pope John Paul stressed the infinite distance between the two principles of time and eternity, between creatures and God. He then went on to show how Jesus made the divine Name his own:

> Existing eternally as the Word, Christ has an origin that goes back far beyond his birth in time. John's assertion is based on Jesus' exact words. To the Jews who rebuked him for claiming to have seen Abraham when he was not yet 50 years old, Jesus replies: 'Truly, truly, I say to you, before Abraham was, I Am' [*Jn* 8:58]. The assertion stressed the contrast between the becoming of Abraham and the being of Jesus.[1]

Pope John Paul commented on the fact that the word *gensthai* used in the Greek text actually means 'to become' or 'to come into being'. It is thus the appropriate verb to use of a creature who comes into existence. It does not possess its existence of itself. In contrast, only Jesus can say 'I am', pointing to the 'fullness of being which lies beyond all becoming. Thus he expresses his awareness of possessing an eternal personal existence'.

The Pope continued:

> By applying the expression 'I am' to himself, Jesus makes God's
> Name his own, the Name revealed to Moses in *Exodus*. After
> entrusting him with the mission of liberating his people from
> slavery in Egypt, Yahweh, the Lord, guarantees him assistance
> and closeness, and in a way as a pledge of his fidelity, he reveals
> to him the mystery of his Name: 'I Am Who I Am' [*Ex* 3:14].
> Thus Moses can say to the Israelites: 'I Am has sent me to you'.
> This Name expresses God's saving presence for the sake of his
> people, but also his inaccessible mystery.[2]

By making the divine Name his own, Our Lord showed us 'that in his
Person eternity not only precedes time, but enters time'.

We can see how Christ's words were a clear claim to divinity, especially
if we translate the words 'before Abraham was' as 'before Abraham came
to be'. The reaction of his adversaries was immediate. They knew the
penalty for blasphemy laid down in *Lev* 24:16: 'Whoever blasphemes the
name of the Lord shall be put to death. The whole community shall stone
him; alien and native alike must be put to death for blaspheming the Lord's
name.' Only Yahweh himself could speak in such terms as he had spoken
to Isaiah: 'I am God, yes, from eternity I am He'. Straightaway, they
seized stones to execute him as one who was guilty of '*Chillul ha-Shem*',
the profanation of the Name.

In fact, this incident in the Temple was but one of numerous occasions
when Christ either explicitly or implicitly applies the words 'I Am Who I
Am' to himself. When Christ walked on the water of the Lake of Galilee,
he reassured the terrified disciples with words that can literally be translated
as 'I Am. Do not be afraid' [*Jn* 6:20]. In the dialogue with the Pharisees
from which the Pope quoted, we also read in the preceding verses:

> 'Therefore I said to you that you will die in your sins; for if you
> do not believe that I am He, you will die in your sins'. Then they
> said to Him, 'Who are you?' And Jesus said to them, 'Just what I
> have been saying to you from the beginning. I have many things
> to say and to judge concerning you, but he who sent me is true;
> and I speak to the world those things which I heard from him.'
> They did not understand that he spoke to them of the Father. Then

Jesus said to them, 'When you lift up the Son of Man, then you will know that I am He, and that I do nothing of myself; but as my Father taught me, I speak these things'. [*Jn* 8:24–28]

At the arrest of Our Lord in Gethsemane, Christ's use of the 'I am' is more ambiguous, but carries great force:

> Jesus therefore, knowing all things that would come upon him, went forward and said to them, 'Whom are you seeking?' They answered him, 'Jesus of Nazareth'. Jesus said to them, 'I am He'. And Judas, who betrayed him, also stood with them. Now when he said to them, 'I am He,' they drew back and fell to the ground. Then he asked them again, 'Whom are you seeking?' And they said, 'Jesus of Nazareth'. Jesus answered, 'I have told you that I am He. Therefore, if you seek Me, let these go their way.' [*Jn* 18:4–8]

At one time, it was the fashion amongst liberal biblical scholars to dismiss St John's Gospel as late and Hellenistic, a view based often on the most flimsy and fragile *a priori* assumptions. Few now would maintain such a view, and the whole thrust of modern Biblical scholarship has been to demonstrate the profoundly Jewish character of John's Gospel, a view that should surprise no one who accepts its Johannine provenance.

That Christ would have made use of the divine Name in order to disclose his divinity would have been the entirely natural mode of expression for himself as a Jew speaking to Jews. In the Scriptures, as we have seen, a name denotes the essential property of the one who bears it. For the Christian, we can see a very close parallel between this idea of God and his Name, and that of the pre-existent Word of God in the prologue to St John's Gospel. In Jewish apocalyptic writings dating from the period 200 BC to 100 AD, visionaries spoke of the Name as the dynamic power of God, his agent in the very act of creation. The *Book of Jubilees* refers to the 'Oath by the glorious, great and mighty Name that made heaven and earth' [36,7].

Much later, in the eighth century, Rabbi Eliezer wrote that 'Before the world was created, only God and his Name existed'. According to Gershom Scholem, some of the Kabbalists maintained that the Name referred to was not simply the Tetragrammaton but the totality of the manifestations of God's power itself. God's Name manifested the totality of his being, but the idea of the pre-existent Name of God was much older, and the parallel with the pre-existent Word, the *logos*, in John is readily apparent.

Once again, we see the profound unity and continuity of the Old and New Testaments. The revelation made to Moses was a revelation of the Word: it was the Son of God who spoke to Moses out of the burning bush, just as the glory of Yahweh that Isaiah had seen in the Temple had been a vision of Christ [cf. *Jn* 12:41]. The God who had promised Moses that he would be with and for his people, now, and in the future as he had been in past, is the 'I am' who is one with Jesus. And for us, what comfort there is in Christ's words as in the words spoken to Isaiah:

> Even to your old age I am the same; even when your hair is grey
> I will bear you. It is I who have done this, I who will continue,
> and I who will carry you to safety. [*Is* 46:4]

The original revelation of the Name to Moses at the burning bush had been above all a revelation of God's 'mercy', of his tender compassion and desire to be with his People. In John's Gospel, the full depth of that mercy is revealed and its implication for those who believe in the Name is made manifest.

Addressing the Father, Christ tells the apostles:

> I made known to them your name and I will make it known, that the
> love with which you loved me may be in them and I in them. And
> now I will no longer be in the world, but they are in the world,
> while I am coming to you. Holy Father, keep them in your name
> that you have given me, so that they may be one just as we are.
> [*Jn* 17:26, 11]

Having received the Name that is above all names, Christ prays that we may be kept in that Name, and that we may be one even as he and the Father are one. Having made known the Name of the Father to the apostles, Christ prays that we may receive the love of the Father, the uncreated Spirit, and that the Son may be in us. The believer is now within the Burning Bush itself, and is not consumed.

A new basis for prayer is announced, prayer in the Name of the Son. This teaching on 'asking in his Name' is clearly inseparable from the promised gift of the Spirit, the Comforter and Consoler, the abiding presence of Jesus with those who call upon his Name. Comfort, consolation and assurance are linked to the great theme of praying in the Name of Our Lord: Christ has revealed and will reveal the Name of the Father to the disciples so that the love with which the Father has loved him may be in them. Again and again, Christ shows us the saving power of his Name and gives us the consoling certitude that our prayer in his Name will be heard:

> And whatever you ask in my name, that I will do, that the Father may be glorified in the Son. If you ask anything in my name, I will do it.  [Jn 14:13–14]

> You did not choose me, but I chose you and appointed you that you should go and bear fruit, and that your fruit should remain, that whatever you ask the Father in my name he may give you. [Jn 15:16]

> And in that day you will ask me nothing. Most assuredly, I say to you, whatever you ask the Father in my name he will give you. Until now you have asked nothing in my name. Ask, and you will receive, that your joy may be full.  [Jn 16:23–24]

This revelation of the Name is made in order that the followers of Jesus may be caught up in the very inner life of God himself: that the love of the Father for the Son may be in them and that the Son may be in them. Christ speaks of having been given the Name of his Father and prays for the apostles that they may be kept in the Name that he has received. This gift of the Name from the Father is a sign of the fact that he and his Father are one [Jn 17:11–12]. In Him, the Name of the Father is glorified [Jn 12:28]. The Father is the Lover, Christ the Beloved and the Holy Spirit is the Love. In Jesus, in his Name, we come to share in that love that created the whole cosmos itself and to behold his glory of the only begotten of the Father, full of grace and truth.

---

1 *L'Osservatore Romano*, n. 49, 3rd December 1997; p. 15.
2 *Ibid.*

# Whoever Calls on the Name of the Lord Shall Be Saved

*A bright light will shine to all the ends of the earth; many nations will come to you from far away, the inhabitants of the remotest parts of the earth to your holy name, bearing gifts in their hands for the King of heaven. Generation after generation will give joyful praise in you, the name of the chosen city will endure forever.* [*Tob* 13:11]

Fifty days after the second day of Passover, the Eleven gathered to celebrate the feast of *Shavuot*, Pentecost, the festival of the wheat harvest. As is attested in the *Book of Jubilees* and the Qumran writings, by the time of Our Lord, Pentecost was seen as a festival of the renewal of the covenant of Sinai and the giving of the *Torah*. It is especially interesting to note that an old Rabbinic tradition extant from the mid-second century, referred to by Rabbi Johanan, states that the revelation of the *Torah* was given in all the languages of mankind, but only the children of Israel accepted it. As God revealed the *Torah*, 'each word which proceeded from the mouth of the Almighty divided into seventy tongues' [*Shab*. 88b], seventy being the traditional number for the languages of the world. At Sinai, one divine voice proclaims the *Torah* in all the languages of the world, but only one people accept it. At Pentecost, the Holy Spirit comes like tongues of fire so that the voices of those gathered in the upper room may proclaim in all the languages of the world that Jesus is Lord.

The theme of harvest recalls Christ's words to his disciples that the harvest is rich but the labourers are few, and that we should pray that the Lord of the harvest send labourers into his harvest. That great harvest begins at Pentecost with the outpouring of the Holy Spirit and the conversion of many people from the different language groups of the world. Pentecost is the day when those who will be labourers in the harvest of the Lord receive the power to proclaim his name throughout all the nations. At Pentecost that harvest begins, with the outpouring of the Holy Spirit, but the harvest continues until the end of time when the final harvest of all will take place, when Christ returns to judge the living and the dead. We receive the fullness of the Holy Spirit at our own Pentecost, when we are confirmed, precisely so that we in our turn may serve as labourers in the harvest of the Lord, and make his Name known.

In Jewish tradition, the Feast of Weeks is linked to the theme of conversion and entry into the people of Israel. On *Shavuot*, the *Book of Ruth* is read in the synagogue, recalling the conversion of the Gentile Ruth to Judaism, a conversion set against the background of the harvest. After the death of her husband, Ruth refuses to return to Moab and begs Naomi:

> Entreat me not to leave you, or to turn back from following after you; for wherever you go, I will go: and wherever you lodge, I will lodge; and your people shall be my people, and your God, my God. [*Ruth* 1:16]

We see how the two ideas of the giving of the *Torah* and the conversion of a Gentile provide a fitting framework for the dramatic events of the first Messianic Pentecost.

At the first *Shavuot* after the Passover of Christ, the Eleven received the gift of the Holy Spirit and began to speak with great power as the Spirit gave them utterance. *Acts* tells us how Jerusalem was full of Jews and proselytes from every linguistic group who had gathered for the festival. They were amazed and perplexed to hear the 'wonderful works of God' proclaimed in their own tongues. Some accused the Apostles of being full of new wine, but Peter raises his voice and tells the crowd that what is happening is the fulfilment of the prophecy of Joel. In the last days God will pour out his Spirit on all flesh, sons and daughters shall prophesy, young men shall see visions and old men shall dream dreams. The quotation culminates in the words: 'And it shall come to pass that whoever calls on the name of the Lord shall be saved' [*Acts* 2:21]. Peter's address to the crowd ends with the invitation:

> Repent and be baptised, every one of you, in the name of Jesus Christ for the forgiveness of your sins; and you will receive the gift of the Holy Spirit. [*Acts* 2:38]

This universality of salvation is the great leitmotif of Acts and is depicted very much in terms of the invocation of the Name being open to all. Not only the sons of Abraham, but all the sons of Noah can receive salvation by invoking the Name of the Lord, and Jesus is both Lord and Messiah. The relationship between Jew and Gentile in the infant Church was a delicate one. At the Council of Jerusalem, the question as to whether or not Gentile converts needed to be circumcised and observe the whole of the *Torah* was resolved. The way in which James answers the debate is highly significant:

> Simon has declared how God first visited the Gentiles to take out of them a people for his Name. And with this the words of the prophets agree, just as it is written: 'After this I will return and will rebuild the tabernacle of David, which has fallen down; I will rebuild its ruins, and I will set it up. So that the rest of mankind may seek the Lord, even all the Gentiles who are called by my Name, says the Lord who does all these things'. [*Acts* 15:14–17, quoting *Amos* 9:11,12]

From the Gentiles, a people has been taken out for the Name: the wild olive tree is grafted on to the holy olive tree of Israel, the people of the Name. The Gentiles too become a people who know the Name.

It is not surprising to learn that some have called *The Acts of the Apostles* the 'Book of the Name' [1]. Rightly so, for again and again the power of the name appears in Luke's narrative. Christ had promised that a new age was coming when people could pray in his Name, and in *Acts* we see lived out in the life and mission of the early Church the sublime truths revealed by Our Lord in his farewell discourse.

Again and again in *Acts*, the power of the Name is made manifest. Peter cures the lame man in the name of Jesus Christ the Nazarene [3:6]. Faith in the Name gives the lame man perfect health and makes him strong [3:16]. There is no other name under heaven given to the human race by which we are to be saved [4:12]. Signs and wonders are done through the name of God's holy servant Jesus [4:30]. After recalling the apostles, the Sanhedrin had them flogged, ordered them to stop speaking in the name of Jesus, and dismissed them [5:40]. Philip preaches the good news about the kingdom of God and the name of Jesus Christ; men and women alike are baptised [8:12]. Converts are baptised in the name of the Lord Jesus [8:16, 10:48, 19:5]. At baptism, his Name is invoked [22:16]. The followers of Jesus are those who call upon his Name [9:14, 21].

Jesus tells Ananias that Paul is 'a chosen instrument of mine to carry my name before Gentiles, kings, and Israelites, and I will show him what he will have to suffer for my name' [9:15–6]. Having previously done many things against the name of Jesus the Nazarene, Paul speaks out boldly in the Name of Jesus [9:27]. Everyone who believes in Jesus will receive forgiveness of sins through his Name [10:43]. The Gentile converts are a people for his Name and those on whom His Name is invoked [15:14, 17]. Paul and Barnabas have dedicated their lives to the name of our Lord Jesus Christ [15:26]. Paul exorcises the girl with a spirit of divination in the name of Jesus Christ, but when itinerant Jewish exorcists attempt to invoke the Name of Jesus without faith there are dire consequences [16:18, 19:13]. Paul states that he is prepared not only to be bound but even to die in Jerusalem for the name of the Lord Jesus [21:13].

In *Acts*, *Kiddush ha-Shem* finds its meaning in the new life of the Christian in Christ, the sanctification of the Name of Jesus. Our English phrase 'in the name of Jesus' does not bring out the richness of the Greek, a richness which reveals the Semitic background of the early Church. In his classic book *The Jesus Prayer*, Lev Gillet wrote:

> In Latin and English the phrase 'in the name of Jesus' is more or less synonymous with 'by the authority of Jesus'; 'in the name of' becomes 'by virtue of'. This is to impoverish the New Testament Greek, stripping it of both its realism and its nuances. The Greek text, when referring to the name of Jesus, uses three formulae: επι τω ονοματι, ειζ το ονομα, εν τω ονοματι. These three formulas are not equivalent, but each one expresses a special attitude towards the name. In επι τω ονοματι one leans *on* the name; it is the foundation on which one builds, the *terminus a quo*, the point of departure toward a subsequent action, the start of a new advance. In ειζ το ονομα, there is a movement *toward* the name, a dynamic relationship of finality which sees the name as a goal to be attained, the *terminus ad quem*. In εν τω ονοματι the attitude is static; it expresses the repose which follows the attainment of the goal and a certain interiorization or immanence; our spirit is transported 'into' the name, within the name, it is united to the name and makes its abode there.[2]

$Ε\iota\zeta$ conveys the idea of moving towards and entering into Christ, $\varepsilon\pi\iota$ of depending upon him, and $\varepsilon v$ the idea of resting and being in Christ. Existentially, the first Christians had discovered the power and the glory of the Name of Jesus.

That burning and exultant note of joy that permeates *Acts* reflects the sense of the first Christians that they were living in the time of fulfilment, when Joel's prophecy was being realised – all men would call on the name of the Lord. At Pentecost, Peter proclaims the fulfilment of this prophecy: the name of Jesus is proclaimed with power, for the risen and exalted Jesus God has made Lord.

Paul sums up the Pentecostal message of hope for all, Jew and Gentile alike, in the injunction: 'For, if you confess with your mouth that Jesus is Lord and believe in your heart that God raised him from the dead, you will be saved' [*Rom* 10:9]. He exhorts the Colossians: 'And whatever you do, in word or in deed, do everything in the name of the Lord Jesus, giving thanks to God the Father through him' [3:17].

This emphasis on thanksgiving and on doing everything in the Name of the Lord Jesus reminds us of the central role of benediction in the spirituality of Judaism, a role that is dealt with at length in the treatise on blessings – *Berakhot* – which is significantly the first tractate in the *Talmud*. The Hebrew noun *berakhah* (plural *berakhot*) is derived from the verb *brkh* ('to fall on one's knees'). Every aspect of life is the subject of a blessing, good or ill, joyful or sad: 'the Lord gives and the Lord takes away, blessed be the Name of the Lord'. To enjoy the blessings of this world without giving blessing is, as it were, to steal from God. The vast array of blessings in the *Talmud*, which cover every aspect of life from seeing the ocean for the first time to the minutiae of daily life, reflects a profound conviction that everything comes from God and returns to God. As priest of creation, man has the God-given duty to give voice to the elemental fact that the Lord our God is the one Lord.

Perhaps this has never been more beautifully expressed than in the words of one of the earliest of all post-Biblical documents, the *Didache*, which dates from the close of the first century, and which may fittingly conclude this chapter on the Name in the young Church:

> We thank you, holy Father, for your sacred Name which you have
> lodged in our hearts, and for the knowledge and faith and

immortality which you have revealed through Jesus, your child. To you be glory forever. Almighty Master, you have created everything for the sake of your Name, and have given people food and drink to enjoy that they may thank you. But to us you have given spiritual food and drink and eternal life through Jesus, your child. Above all, we thank you that you are mighty. To you be glory forever. Remember, Lord, your Church, to save it from all evil and to make it perfect by your love. Make it holy, and gather it together from the four winds into your Kingdom which you have made ready for it. For yours is the power and the glory forever. Let Grace come and let this world pass away. Hosanna to the God of David. If anyone is holy, let him come. If not, let him repent. Our Lord, come! Amen.[3]

1  e.g. L Gillett (a Monk of the Orthodox Church), *The Jesus Prayer*, revised edition with a foreword by Kallistos Ware, Bishop of Diokleia, Crestwood, New York, 1997; p. 27.
2  Ibid., p. 27.
3  B D Ehrman, *The New Testament and Other Early Christian Writings: A Reader*, Oxford, 1997; p. 316.

# On Language and the Name

*For then I will restore to the peoples a pure language,*
*that they all may call on the name of the Lord,*
*to serve him with one accord.*  [*Zeph* 3:9]

Like the potter and his clay, language moulds us. We are what we say and what we hear. Without language, we can barely think. Language is our interface with the world and it is difficult for us even to imagine human life without words. Indeed, some linguists have gone so far as to argue that we live only in that part of the world that our language allows us to know. We live by words, by embodied thoughts that enable us to have a fully conscious awareness not only of the external world but also of our own interior selves.

In the *Tractatus Logico-philosophicus*, the early Wittgenstein maintained that the frontiers of our language are the frontiers of our world, and held that 'What we cannot say we cannot know'. But in human experience, we are conscious of the fact that very often the real problem is that we cannot say what we do know. All too often we are painfully aware of the limitations of speech, and of how we cannot put into words all that we think and feel. When we need them most, words fail us. We know their deceptiveness and ambiguity: words mask as well as reveal our thought. Our souls long for a speech that will not bear false witness to what is within us. Even our own native tongue can be a frail and imperfect thing. Compared to the reality, the greatest poem is a thing of straw and our hearts hunger for a purer speech, for a holy tongue.

The sheer abundance and diversity of human language is an almost unfathomable mystery. Although the number of languages in the world is sadly declining, there are still some four to five thousand different languages, leaving aside dialects. The curious thing is that very often the older the language, the more complicated it is. In Pais Vasco in Spain and in the Pays Basque in France, for example, some 500,000 people speak Basque, a linguistic isolate which has its origins in prehistory. Basque appears to be totally unrelated to any other language and is so impenetrable as to be virtually unlearnable by those who did not learn it from the cradle.

Aymara, one of the Andean-Equatorial languages, going back in time to before the Incas, has been hailed by some linguists as a perfect language because of its almost boundless subtlety, flexibility and ability to convey the most abstruse of abstract thoughts. Truly, the great feast of languages is one of the most amazing facts about our human condition.

On one level, the existence of such a multiplicity of languages can so easily create barriers to mutual understanding, that lead to bitter conflict and dispute. On a deeper level, however, each language is much more than a means of conveying information. Language expresses and embodies something very precious and special in the human spirit. It is part of the richness and exuberance of life. Each language has its own unique insight into the world and, as the Welsh saying goes, 'a nation without a language is a nation without a heart'. Imagine, for example, a group of children being asked to draw a house and each child given a different coloured crayon. The same house would be drawn but each picture would be unique. In the same way, human language is much more than some linguistic binary code, and the death of any language diminishes us all. To lose a language is to lose a colour from the spectrum or to watch a rainbow fade. It is said that those who are the last speakers of an ancient language suffer from a sense of almost unimaginable despair and isolation.

This richness of languages becomes apparent when we reflect on the unspoken associations and meaning of the words we use. We discover that there are words in one language that are not properly translatable into another. There is no exact equivalent. Vocabulary is only a small part of the problem, but it is a significant one. Umberto Eco cited an interesting example when he noted that Italian has no word that is directly equivalent as such to our English 'to skip'or 'to hop'.[1] We all know the difficulties posed for Westerners who seek to understand Japanese honorifics. Then there are all of the emotional evocations of words: a 'maison' is not a 'home'. The Welsh *hiraeth* is much more acute and specific than the English words 'longing' or 'nostalgia'. Perhaps more than any other language, Yiddish has a tremendous subtlety and expressiveness in conveying family and inter-personal relationships, humour and irony, which accounts for its having become such a fertile quarry for providing loan words into English. Each language embodies the unique historical and cultural experience of the community that speaks it and hence translation from one language into another is always to some extent a translation of poetry into prose.

On a deeper level than vocabulary, a Semitic language such as Hebrew reflects a radically different linguistic structure from that of a modern Western language. Without wishing to push this too far, since translation *is* possible, such linguistic differences are indicative to a certain degree of a different way of looking at the world. Hebrew's verbal system is based not on a distinction of time as in a Western language, which has a 'one-way street' and linear view of time with past, present and future tenses. Instead, Hebrew is more concerned with distinctions of state of being, complete or incomplete, single or repeated, lasting or instantaneous.

In many ways, it could be said that the Hebrew view better represents our true experience of time in which past, present and future have to be set in the context of God's creative Word, where time began and where time will end. Rabbi Lawrence Kushner wrote:

> There are two ways of experiencing the flow of time. In contemporary secular time, time is infinitely and irreversibly linear. It is without beginning or end. And since no two moments ever coincide, each minute, day, week, and year must have its unique number.
>
> In religious time, on the other hand, the flow of time began with God's word and likewise will end with his word. And within these two termini there are identical circles of time. Some are larger, some smaller. There are weeks, each ending with a Sabbath. But every Sabbath is identical to every other Sabbath even as they are all like the Sabbath on which 'God rested from all his work that he had done'. Holy time does not march on. Once the candles are lit there is no 'next' *Shabbos*.[2]

When, for instance, we say in English 'Do this in memory of me,' almost inevitably our linguistic thought-forms suggest the idea of doing an action simply to recall an event that is over and done with in the past. We tend to see the past in rigid compartments and segments, in a highly analytical way. For us, 'memory' carries with it the association of separation from an event or person, a gap that we seek to alleviate by recalling the past. All we have are our memories. But the Semitic view of the Bible is very different: the very structure of the language can evoke the past as an ongoing event in the present and continuing into the future.

In Hebrew and Aramaic, Hebrew's cousin language, time past and time future are both present in time now. Thus the Passover Seder celebrates not just what happened over three thousand years to the Israelites: all those who celebrate it now, celebrate their own deliverance from bondage. This applies with even greater force to the Mass where Christ himself comes among us as Priest and Victim. The Hebrew and Aramaic imperfect tense conveys the idea of God's continuing action stretching back to the past and into the future with both meeting in the present. Consequently, Hebrew can express certain subtle distinctions difficult to convey in any European language, and yet Hebrew lacks the vast wealth of English adjectives – which is why we have such distinctive phrases in the Scriptures as 'Holy of holies' and 'King of kings'. It is also a language of the concrete and physical as even the aesthetics of the Hebrew script itself suggest.

Although we rejoice at the wonderful variety of the myriad languages of the world, we are also acutely aware of the need for a unifying common language and of the limitations of existing languages. The philosopher Leibnitz dreamed of creating a language that would be 'an algebra of thought'. In the nineteenth century, Zamenhof devised Esperanto as a universal auxiliary language in the hope, as its name suggests, that it could lessen the misunderstandings that lead to war. This hope for the future corresponds to an intuitive belief expressed in myth and legend that humanity's division into so many linguistic groups was not so in the beginning.

The legend of a holy tongue, the 'lingua Adamica' – the lost universal language of mankind – has haunted mankind since the dawn of history. In the fifth century BC, Herodotus described an attempt made by the Egyptian king Psamtik I two centuries before his own time to discover the oldest language. The Babel legend is paralleled in many diverse and separate cultures, even in the Mayan civilisation of central America. The *Popul Vuh* tells of the building of the great pyramid of Cholula, as a refuge from flooding, and how, after its construction, its builders were scattered and their speech divided. Jewish Kabbalists taught that this vanished tongue had mystical properties. In this language God spoke to Adam and Adam named the animals. It was the medium that expressed man's stewardship over the earth, his God-given suzerainty over creation. St Augustine saw in this naming of the animals a sign of the transcendental wisdom given to Adam at his fashioning from the earth. Possibly Augustine derived this view from the Latin version of the Scriptures, which has Adam call the animals *nominibus suis* (by their own names), suggesting a special insight into the mind of the supreme Name-Giver, God himself. Knowledge of this language enabled man to share in God's own creative work.

Medieval theologians reflected on Adam's preternatural mental abilities by which his mind could move instantly from physical object to intellectual concept. Unlike our modern, broken tongues, the language of Eden mapped reality, with a perfect correspondence between 'verbum' (word) and 'res' (thing). In it, meaning and expression were transparent. The 'holy tongue' was analogous to angelic speech. St Thomas Aquinas held that angelic speech is a direct communication of knowledge from spirit to spirit, although not in sounds or uttered words. Paradise language reflected the elevated state of nature before the Fall. Its loss at Babel was among the greatest catastrophes to befall humanity. Already barred from Paradise by the flaming sword, the descendants of Adam and Eve are now cast out from communion with their own kind. Every man's hand is against his brother.

Philologists have pursued that lost first language, the so-called *Ur-Sprache*, like the Holy Grail. Before the hypothetical Nostratic language, itself going back to the last Ice Age some 15,000 years ago, and the supposed ancestor of Indo-European, Kartvelian, Afro-Asiatic, Uralic, Dravidian and Altaic families, lies that vanished tongue. Some linguists, notably Merritt Ruhlen and John D Bengston, have even posited a hypothetical 'Proto-World' language. They have suggested some 45 global etymologies based on cognate words common to the hypothetical linguistic macro-families of Nostratic, Eurasiatic, Amerind and Dene-Sino-Caucasian. If they are right, then just possibly some of the words as far back as Paleolithic times are startingly familiar: *tik* (finger, digit, one), *aq'wa* (water), *mano* (man), *maco* (child) and *maliqa* (milk).

The linguistic theories of Ruhlen and Bengston are still very far from gaining general acceptance, but they do reflect a perennial human interest in the origins of human language. Perhaps fragments of this *Ur-Sprache* do indeed survive, buried like the oldest rock beneath all the accumulated strata heaped upon it since, but we shall never know. After so many millennia, we cannot hope to rediscover it: it remains forever beyond the horizon and shrouded in mystery.[3]

What we do know is that the origins of human language are very ancient indeed, going back possibly as far as 200,000 years to mitochondrial Eve in Africa. Language and thought are so inter-dependent that we find it hard to imagine man without language. In the deep structures of the mind, human beings have an inner propensity for language. Man is *homo loquens*. He is man the talker.

The Biblical view is of a linguistic catastrophe at the very dawn of human history, a catastrophe that mirrors the loss of Eden and the sin of Cain. The story of Babel is not an exercise in scientific historical philology but the inspired author does express in solemn and poetic words the truth and meaning of language. Before Babel, there was one language alone, spoken and understood by all.[4] With the confusion of men's speech, each man becomes isolated: dialogue degenerates into monologue, and each man's hand is set against his brother.

The loss of that language becomes a mythic symbol of the loss of Paradise. Once, man conversed openly and fully with God and his fellow man. Then that language was lost, and the languages that have come since – so glorious and so diverse – are but shards of shattered glass, reflecting the light but no longer the meaning. The glass of the lamp has been broken.

Some religious writers tried to guess at what that first language was like. They speculated on its relationship to Hebrew, the first language of revelation, and argued that here and there a word may survive the wreck. But the glass can never be put back together. The holy tongue once heard on the lips of men is now lost. It is forever beyond our grasp, like the forgotten lines of Coleridge's *Xanadu* or music heard in a dream that fades on waking. The Kabbalists believed that what was lost was much more than a mere *lingua franca*, a simple means of communication based on a shared knowledge of one limited language. Eden's language mirrored as in a glass the very speech of God himself, thus becoming a vehicle for the communication of the secret of the universe itself. It was the language of vision and miracle, where word and thought were one, and where the name of the rose and the rose were one.

Of course, many will dismiss the religious search for the holy tongue as a simple nostalgia for paradise, for a glory that has passed away. Modern philologists are, of course, correct in saying that there is no reason for believing that the first language had either mystical or occult powers. Nonetheless, we can say theologically that the first speech would, however, have possessed an integrity lacking in our modern speech, not because of any inherent magical power, but because of the state of grace of those who spoke it, no matter how limited linguistically as a language that first speech may have been. It is the Spirit that gives life: the flesh is of no avail.

Before the Fall, in the state of original justice, language possessed sincerity and a truth not readily found in our modern speech, not through any intrinsic property of its own, but simply because our speech is bent and corrupted by our self-seeking and sin. What is sought in the past is to be found in the future. The anguish and the pain that comes from the memory of what is lost and is forever out of reach is healed by our hope in what is to come.

Here, there is a deeper truth. The longing for the lost tongue, the holy speech, is for something that cannot be fulfilled by any human language. But that yearning for a golden age should not be dismissed therefore as some romantic escapism from the cares of the present, this vale of tears. As Cardinal Newman observed, the nostalgia for Paradise that is a part of the universal human condition is in reality a longing after the future, for a glorious restoration that surpasses that which was lost:

> They think that they regret the past when they are but longing for the future. It is not that they would be children again but that they would be angels and would see God: they would be immortal beings, crowned with amaranth, robed in white, and with palms in their hands, before his throne.[5]

This longing for heaven helps us to understand why Pentecost is much more than a simple reversal of the tragedy of Babel. No restoration of some long lost primordial language from the dawn of history could possibly restore unity to mankind. The reconstruction of the Palaeolithic language of our first ancestors would merely add to the languages of the world. The Apostles did not begin to speak the language of Eden at Pentecost but 'in other tongues, as the Spirit gave them utterance'. Devout men 'from every nation under earth' heard them proclaiming in their own tongues the mighty works of God.

The picture here is not the restoration of a prehistoric language but the transfiguration and transformation of language itself. Each language becomes a 'holy tongue', precisely because at Pentecost it becomes a medium for the communication of the Holy Spirit. Human languages rediscover their source in God, begin to serve his kingdom and to plant their roots in the new Paradise. They are a part of a world redeemed.

On Calvary, the Good Thief called on Jesus to remember him when he came into his kingdom, and Christ promised him Paradise. Now, when the Name of Jesus is invoked, in all the languages of the world, the gate to Paradise is opened and the flaming sword is removed. The sword of the Spirit now ushers in a new and more glorious Eden, the life of Heaven itself. The tree of the cross is the new tree of life from which all may freely eat because Christ gives us new life in his Name.

This life is made present at the foundation of the Church and remains present eternally. As the soul of the Church, Christ's Body, the Holy Spirit works to fashion a new human solidarity in Christ, the Second Adam, a human unity in a diversity of persons that is an image of the life of the Trinity. Necessarily, this means a new speech.

The Apostles gathered in the room at Pentecost. Suddenly a sound came from heaven like the rush of a mighty wind, filling the house where they were sitting. Tongues of fire appeared resting on each of them. Filled with the Holy Spirit, they began to speak in other tongues, with utterance given by the Spirit. People from different nations heard them speaking, each in their native tongue. At the revelation of the Name, Moses looked on the burning bush from outside, but now the tongues of fire rest on the Apostles, and they are not consumed. The fire of the Holy Spirit is within them.

The encounter with the sacred is always an invitation for us to enter into a dialogue. We feel in the very core of our being the call to respond to the awe-inspiring mystery before us. We sense not some blind, impersonal force, but a person, a Thou. Once we begin to speak of a Thou, we are speaking of names, of language and of relationships. In fear and trembling, man asks the name of God that he might know and adore him. Thus, as the dawn broke, Jacob asked the name of the mysterious stranger with whom he had wrestled all night by the ford of the brook Jabbok. Our sense of the numinous leads us into the world of dialogue, although we are in the area of that which totally transcends our finite being.

Words, names and language enable us to enter into a relationship with persons. Language itself is based on a dialogue between an 'I' and a 'Thou,' with what is expressed, what is communicated, as the link between speaker and hearer. Language itself is thus Trinitarian. A dynamic bond is created by that exchange between the caller and the one who is called, and calls in return. This triune structure of language takes on even greater force when we remember that in Hebrew the same word *dabar* represents both 'word' and 'thing'. The 'word' is not just a symbol of thought. In an imperfect and analogous way, human language is an icon of the ecstatic Triune life of God himself, who is One but not solitary.

The primary purpose of creation is the revelation of God's glory: the visible creation reflects the glory of the invisible Father whom no man has ever seen, the God who utterly transcends all human sight. God's creation of the cosmos is both the condition and the means by which the Incarnation itself is made possible. It is a condition, for without the creation of a reality distinct from God there could be no Incarnation. It is a means because it is through that God-given reality that the uncreated Word takes flesh in the womb of the Virgin Mary. In this sense, we can truly say that the universe was made so that the child might be born in Bethlehem.

Christ comes to glorify the Name of his Father. He is the perfect revelation of the Father, the eternal High Priest who gathers all things in himself and enables man to fulfil his destiny as priest of creation – to be the voice of creation itself. The very act of creation is itself an act of divine communication, and what is true of the visible creation applies also to the audible creation.

At a General Audience on 20 February 1980, Pope John Paul said:

> The body, in fact, and it alone, is capable of making visible what is invisible: the spiritual and the divine. It was created to transfer to the visible reality of the world the invisible mystery hidden since time immemorial in God, and thus be a sign of it.

Human language, frail and imperfect as it is, can likewise bring to the audible reality of the world the inaudible mystery of the eternal Word. God's words in Scripture are thus an icon of the ineffable Word of God, leading us into the silence of contemplation, where we go beyond our human speech and enter into the very language of God himself.

The Spirit at Pentecost comes to draw us into the life of the God who is Three in One. In *Genesis*, after the Fall, we read of Enoch and how 'at that time men began to call upon the name of the Lord'. As a consequence of the Fall, language carried within itself the seeds of division and conflict, but language itself was not lost. God did not take language itself from man and thus reduce him to the state of the dumb beasts. At Babel, the holy tongue was lost and the unity of mankind fragmented. Nonetheless, language still survived as a medium for God's revelation and as an agent of human solidarity. The image remained but the likeness was lost.

When men gathered on the plain of Shinar, they still spoke the same language with the same words. There they built a town and a tower with its top reaching to heaven. Their aim was to make a name for themselves, so that they might not be scattered about the whole earth. It was the old sin of rebellion, of disobedience, of 'I will not serve', because man names all other creatures but God alone gives man his name. To seek a name for oneself and to reject the name given by God is to want to place oneself, not God, at the centre. This false name is conceived of in terms of self-glory and pride. The perpetuation of one's name is here part of a desire to cheat death itself, with the name as a memorial seen as a means of achieving immortality. Again, man reaches out to eat of the tree of the knowledge of good and evil, and to usurp the throne of God himself.

The new Adam, Christ, does not ascend to heaven by means of any titanic attempt to storm heaven by building a tower. He ascends by coming down, by emptying himself, taking the form of a servant and our human nature to himself. Christ humbles himself and becomes obedient unto death, even death on a cross, and therefore God has exalted him and bestowed on him the Name that is above every name.

Dominion over all languages and tongues is a sign of the coming of the Son of Man who ushers in the Kingdom of God. The prophet Daniel was watching in the night visions, and behold, one like the Son of Man, coming with the clouds of heaven! He came to the Ancient of Days, and they brought him near before him. Then to him was given dominion and glory and a kingdom, that all peoples, nations, and languages should serve him. His dominion is an everlasting dominion, which shall not pass away, and his kingdom the one which shall not be destroyed.  [*Dan* 7:13–14]

At Pentecost, as Peter says, the prophecy of Joel is fulfilled regarding the last day: 'And it shall be that whoever calls on the name of the Lord shall be saved'.

On the night of his betrayal, along with the Eucharist and the priesthood, Our Lord gives us prayer in his Name: 'Truly, truly, I say to you, if you ask anything of the Father he will give it to you in my name. Hitherto you have asked nothing in my name; ask, and you will receive, that your joy may be complete'. He tells the disciples of the coming of the Counsellor, the Holy Spirit, whom the Father will send in his name.

At Pentecost, human languages achieve their ultimate purpose of invoking the name of the Lord: the name of Jesus is the meaning and purpose of all human speech. The prophecy of Zephaniah is fulfilled:

> At that time I will change the speech of the peoples to a pure speech, that all of them may call on the name of the Lord and serve him with one accord. [*Zeph* 3:9]

This creation of a pure speech is the reversal of Babel. The pure speech is given so that all peoples may call on the Name of the Lord and serve him as one.

We see just how revolutionary all this is when we set Peter's Pentecostal proclamation of the Name against the background of contemporary Judaism which restricted the vocalisation of the Name of Yahweh to one man, and then only on one day of the year. Once a year, in the Temple, within the Holy of Holies on the Day of Atonement, the High Priest alone was permitted to utter the great and all-holy Name of God. Even then, by the time of the coming of the Messiah, this Name was already held to be so sacred that it was pronounced only by the High Priest and, even then, was drowned by the music of the Levites lest the Name be profaned. As the High Priest spoke, the people responded: 'Blessed be the Name; the glory of his Kingdom is for ever and ever'.

Gradually, a whole mysticism of the Name developed. In the *Berit Menuhah*, a 14th-century work on the Tetragrammaton, Abraham of Granada stated that this uttering of the Name in the Temple was a moment of such overwhelming majesty and divine power that the very existence of the universe depended upon it. If the High Priest had lingered over long on a consonant or mispronounced it, the world itself would have ceased to endure. The very continuance of the universe hung in the balance, the Temple threshold trembled and the light of the Shekhinah filled the Temple.

Pentecost is the fulfilment of Joel's prophecy and Peter quotes his words:

> And afterward, I will pour out my Spirit on all people. Your sons and daughters will prophesy, your old men will dream dreams, your young men will see visions. Even on my servants, both men and women, I will pour out my Spirit in those days. I will show wonders in the heavens and on the earth, blood and fire and billows of smoke. The sun will be turned to darkness and the moon to blood before the coming of the great and dreadful day of the Lord. And everyone who calls on the name of the Lord will be saved. [*Joel* 2:28–32]

To call on the Name of the Lord was to come into the presence of the thrice-holy Lord of hosts whose glory fills the whole earth. As St John tells us, the vision Isaiah had in the Temple was a vision of Christ.

Now Christ has entered, not into a sanctuary made with human hands, a shadow and a copy of the true one, but into heaven itself. In him, the whole of humanity, Jew and Gentile, male and female, slave and free, can call on the Name of the Lord. All who have been baptised into Christ's death and resurrection become members of a new and royal priesthood. All have entry to the innermost sanctuary where they can call on the Name of the Lord. The Name of the Lord is no longer known only by the High Priest to be uttered once a year. It is on our lips, it is in our mind, and it is in our heart. In Jesus, we see and touch the glory of the secret Name of God that is one with the divine essence itself and thus transcends the whole of creation.

In the prayer of the heart, in the prayer of the Church, language itself is transfigured. The veil of the Temple separating God and man, and man from his fellow man is no more. Such prayer is a foretaste of that moment of daybreak for which our hearts long so greatly, when we shall call on his Name and hear his voice, as he calls us by our own truest and innermost name. Then we shall see him face to face and be plunged into a bliss beyond all human words when the Lord himself shall be the Name we speak, and there shall be a new heaven and a new earth.

---

1 Umberto Eco, *The Search for the Perfect Language*, Oxford, 1995; pp 349–350.

2 L Kushner, *Honey from the Rock: Visions of Jewish Mystical Renewal*, Woodstock, Vermont, 1990; pp. 79–80.

3 Sumerian is the oldest recorded written language and dates from the fourth millennium before Christ. It is a linguistic isolate unrelated to any other known language. Possibly Basque, another linguistic isolate, has the strongest claim to be the most ancient language still spoken within Europe. Famously, the Basque words for axe or knife (*haizkora* and *haiztoa*) are derived from the word *haitz*, which means 'cutting-rock' or 'stone', and may reflect (at least for these words) an ancestry of words that goes back to Neolithic times, before the coming of the Indo-Europeans. Could Basque contain the last faint echoes of the speech of the cave painters of Lascaux? The majority opinion among linguists would be that all languages (including Basque) have so metamorphosed over the course of history that any talk of reconstructing the language of man before mankind came 'out of Africa' is meaningless. It is, however, by no means improbable that the remote language 'super-families' from which the extant languages of the world are descended may in their turn demonstrate certain common features that provide a tantalising glimpse of that first language of *Homo Sapiens*.

4 Common Rabbinic opinion was that this one language was in fact Hebrew, to which Jews alone remained faithful. In the Messianic age, the language of all peoples will once again be Hebrew, the holy tongue. This is why some ultra-Orthodox groups refuse to use Hebrew in everyday speech in present-day Israel, because to do so would be to anticipate the coming of the Messiah. They use Yiddish, the 'mother tongue,' which has acquired a new status as the language of the martyrs since the Holocaust. Although recognising the special status of Hebrew and Greek as languages of revelation, Christians have had from the beginning what one might term a 'vernacular' approach. In the mid-third century, Origen wrote: 'Christians in prayer do not even use the precise names that divine Scripture applies to God. Rather, the Greeks use Greek names. The Romans use Latin names. And

everyone prays and sings praises to God as best he can in his mother tongue. For the Lord of all the languages of the earth hears those who pray to him in each different language' (quoted in D W Bercot (ed.), *A Dictionary of Early Christian Beliefs*, Hendrickson (Peabody, Massachusetts), 1998; page 314). The use of 'Yeshua' by modern Messianic Jews for 'Jesus' is a sign of their faith as Jewish Christians, and they do not seek to impose this usage on Gentile believers.

5 *Parochial and Plain Sermons*, IV, 17.

# The Written Name

*Pilate answered, 'What I have written, I have written'.*
*[Jn 19:22]*

It is simply to state the obvious to say that we know far more about the appearance of Julius Caesar or the Emperor Tiberius than we do about that of Our Lord. Indeed, we know next to nothing about Christ's appearance. Just possibly he may have looked older than his true age, a deduction based on the charge of the Pharisees that Our Lord was not yet 50 and yet claimed to have seen Abraham. Possibly Our Lord looked nearer 50 than 33. But such hypothetical speculation does not remotely amount to what we could properly call a description.

As far as we know, no artist ever painted a portrait of Christ. Given Our Lord's lowly social status, it would have been most unlikely that any such portrait would have been made. Of course, unconsciously we all assume that we know what Christ looked like, because we are so conditioned to seeing him depicted in works of art. However, such works of art represent only artists' impressions. Even though there are many cogent reasons for accepting the authenticity of the Turin Shroud, it still remains the object of scientific debate.

In the modern Western world, the visual image is so ubiquitous that it dominates our perception to the exclusion of all other modes of apprehension. The plain truth is that God wishes us to look not with the eyes of the flesh but with the eyes of faith. Revelation is by the Word, not by picture, statue or photograph. In fact, it is the recognition of this truth that gives the icons of the Eastern Church their great power and special value: they give a visual expression to the faith of the Church rather than vainly attempting to provide a portrait of the Lord. Icons are indeed the Gospels in paint.

Before the first icon was made, the Name of Our Lord was written. The *Catechism* tells us that the 'name is the icon of the person' [2158] and hence is holy. This holiness of the name is not limited to the spoken name, but also extends to the written name.

The ancient world did not draw the hard and fast distinction between the written and the spoken word that we do in modern times. One of the most famous examples of this is to be found in the *Acts of the Apostles*, when Philip is on the desert road from Jerusalem to Gaza and meets the Ethiopian eunuch. The eunuch is in his chariot, reading the book of Isaiah. Philip runs up to the chariot and hears the eunuch reading, for it was the normal practice in the ancient world to read aloud. The library of Alexandria would have been a noisy place. The spoken and written word were always linked, and this extended obviously to the spoken and the written name.

The first references to the written Name of Jesus occur in the Passion narratives. All four Passion narratives refer to the inscription Pilate ordered to be placed above the head of Christ on the Cross. There are apparent discrepancies in the wording of the inscription given by the four evangelists. Not unsurprisingly it is John, who stood at the foot of the cross, who gives the fullest version of the text, and he alone gives us the information that the inscription was trilingual:

> Pilate also had an inscription written and put on the cross. It read, 'Jesus the Nazarene, the King of the Jews'. Now many of the Jews read this inscription, because the place where Jesus was crucified was near the city; and it was written in Hebrew, Latin, and Greek. [*Jn* 19:20]

Bearing in mind what we have already said about the lack of distinction between the spoken and the written word, the onlookers would probably have read the words out loud, thus unknowingly proclaiming the kingship of Christ, and this would have greatly angered the religious authorities, who protested to Pilate.

From John's Gospel we derive the familiar abbreviation 'INRI', 'Iesus Nazarenus Rex Iudaeorum', often placed on crucifixes. It was common Roman practice to attach a board to the cross, bearing the details of the charge against the person being crucified. The inscription, known as the 'titulus', would have been of sufficient size for the lettering on it to be read by the spectators. Often these 'titles' were in more than one language. A modern parallel can be found in the Soviet Union during the Second World War: Nazi death squads placed placards around the necks of their victims when they hanged them, with the word 'partisan' written on them in German and Cyrillic Russian script.

The chief priests protested to Pilate that he should have written, 'he claimed to be the king of the Jews' rather than 'the king of the Jews'. From Pilate's reply, 'What I have written, I have written', it would seem possible that Pilate himself as Roman governor had written the judgement, perhaps in Greek as well as Latin, to be copied out by a sign-writer. He may then have ordered that his words be translated also into Hebrew or Aramaic. Since this was the language of the people, it would have contained the fullest details of the charge and would, in Pilate's mind, have been the most mocking.

What Pilate did not realise was that the words he intended as mockery were quite simply the literal truth – Jesus of Nazareth *was* the King of the Jews. Just as Caiaphas had not realised the prophetic force of his words when he told the Sanhedrin that it was expedient for one man to die for the nation, so Pilate did not realise the force of his words 'Jesus the Nazarene, the king of the Jews'. The chief priests wanted the words 'He said, "I am the King of the Jews" ' substituted for 'The King of the Jews', but Pilate replied 'What I have written, I have written': neither the name nor the title of Jesus was to be erased. Pilate did not know it, but he was in fact acting in accordance with Jewish law that forbade the erasing of the Name of God.

The image of the cross is thus, for all eternity, linked with the image of the Name of Jesus. Crucified between two criminals, Jesus was numbered with sinners and, in fulfilment of the prophecy of Zechariah, men looked on the one they had pierced. The one they had pierced was Adonai himself:

> And I will pour out on the house of David and the inhabitants of Jerusalem a spirit of grace and supplication. They will look on me, the one they have pierced, and they will mourn for him as one mourns for an only child, and grieve bitterly for him as one grieves for a firstborn son. [*Zech* 12:10 (NIV)]

In his classic book *Jesus the Messiah*, Alfred Edersheim argued convincingly that the variations in the wording of the inscription in the four Gospels go back to the inscription itself.[1] Matthew's version gives us a translation of the Latin text, 'This is Jesus the King of the Jews', Latin being the language of the Roman imperial authority. Mark gives us the Greek text, 'The King of the Jews', with Luke giving the slight variant of 'This is the King of the Jews' or, possibly, just giving the second half of the Aramaic text. Greek was the *lingua franca* of the Hellenistic world. John gives us a translation of the Aramaic or Hebrew text, the language of the Jews: 'Jesus the Nazarene, the king of the Jews'. The sacred text of the Scripture itself, of course, gives the Name of Jesus in Greek.[2]

The Name of the Messiah is holy in all languages, but it is to be regretted that almost all crucifixes give only the abbreviations of the Latin title on the cross. The full trilingual inscription is seldom if ever reproduced, and partly as a consequence of this, the form of 'Yeshua' is not as widely known as it should be. In each language, the Name manifests the presence of the saving Lord. Above the crown of thorns, the Name is written: Yahweh is with his People.

In all the languages of the world, the Name of Jesus is a *nomen sacrum*, a 'holy name'. From the earliest times, Christian scribes often wrote the name of Jesus in an abbreviated form, along with words such as 'God', 'Lord' and 'Christ', in conscious emulation of the Jewish custom of using the Hebrew alphabet when writing the name of Yahweh in Greek manuscripts. In a Hebrew text, there are, of course, no true vowels. Although writing in Greek, the early scribes imported this practice in a modified form into the Greek text by very often deliberately omitting the vowels of the Greek stem. Sometimes the scribes would omit some of the consonants. The special contracted form of a 'holy name' was then indicated by placing a line above the letter or letters involved, a practice that was used normally to distinguish letters used as numbers. The 'sacred name' thus stood out clearly in the main body of the written text. In *The Letter of Barnabas*, the writer refers to the contracted form 'IH', a *nomen sacrum* for Jesus, and to its numerical value of 18, which is perhaps best known in its Hebrew form of *chai*, which means 'life'.

This Jewish practice had the effect of visually heightening the sacred Name by introducing Hebrew consonants into a Greek text. The use of abbreviations for sacred names in Christian manuscripts in Greek was not motivated by economic questions of saving papyrus by employing shorthand, but rather by a desire to emphasise the holiness of the Name. The Name of Jesus is more than a sacred name: it is a divine Name.

There is a message here for us nearly two millennia later. We are so accustomed to writing the Name of the Lord, almost without thinking, as if it were the same as any other name. There is something that we can learn from the reticence and awe of these first Christian scribes. To write the Name of Jesus is an act of faith in the whole mystery of the Incarnation and redemption. The hallowing of the Name of God must extend not only to the spoken Name but also to the written Name.

In the Middle Ages, devotion to the visible Name took a tangible form, largely as a result of the zeal of the Franciscan Order. When preaching, St Bernardine of Siena (1380–1444) exhibited a board in a gilt frame on which was painted the Name of Jesus, surrounded by twelve rays of the sun. Normally, St Bernardine used the abbreviated form 'IHS' written in Gothic letters; a monogram derived from the first three letters of the Greek form of Jesus. A tiny cross generally surmounted the letter 'H'. Many of these plaques were in fact made by a former manufacturer of playing cards in Bologna, whom Bernardine had put out of business by his highly effective attacks on the evils of gambling.

A tireless missioner, Bernardine travelled the length and breadth of Italy on foot, constantly preaching, with such great effect that Pius II was to call him a second St Paul. With the help of his friend, St John of Capistrano, St Bernardine promulgated devotion to the Holy Name in its written form. Initially, he met with opposition from some quarters, and his detractors accused him of heresy. His critics particularly objected to the saint's practice of exposing the monogram at the end of his sermons, and then exhorting his listeners to kneel with him and to worship their Saviour. In 1427, Pope Martin V cleared Bernardine of the charges of heresy and idolatry that had been brought against him. By his own personal example, the Pope endorsed the practice of venerating the monogram by taking part in a procession in which the IHS symbol was carried in procession. Five years later, Pope Eugenius issued a bull endorsing the devotion to the written Name. From then on, the devotion spread rapidly throughout the Church: the IHS monogram became universally known throughout the western Church, even appearing on watermarks in paper.

As so often with the Franciscans, Bernardine possessed a special charism of going to the heart of the Gospel. Significantly, the sacred monogram is linked with the Cross, and we can see the scriptural echo here of the first inscription to bear the Name of the Lord. Largely as a result of Bernardine's preaching, devotion to the written Name spread throughout the late medieval world and was hugely popular. He played an important part in promoting the inclusion of the Holy Name in the 'Hail Mary'. Later, the Jesuits adopted the 'IHS' monogram and further promulgated it throughout the Church. To this day, the monogram is often stamped on the altar breads that are to be changed into the Body of Christ.

Towards the end of the fifteenth century, various masses of the Holy Name appeared in some dioceses in Germany, Scotland, England, Spain, and Belgium, with the authority of local bishops. Clement VII in 1530 approved an Office and Mass composed by Bernardine dei Busti (d. 1500), for use in Franciscan churches. Gradually the Feast of the Holy Name spread throughout much of the Church and was finally made universal by Pope Innocent XIII in 1721, at the request of the Emperor Charles VI. The feast was suppressed in 1969 but continues in the Roman Missal as a votive Mass.

Constantly extolling the beauty and power of the name of Jesus, St Bernardine had a burning zeal to see the holy name or one of its abbreviations inscribed on the external and internal walls of both public buildings and private houses. Bernardine persuaded many to display the monogram in public places, on altars and on the walls of churches. He was especially insistent on the importance of having the IHS placed above the main door of the house, an interesting but unconscious parallel to the placing of the mezuzah in the Jewish faith. The monogram with the intertwined letters IHS can still be seen on many doorways in Siena. His initial motive may have been to replace the political slogans of the rival Guelph and Ghibelline parties with the Name that fostered harmony. But, when one reads Bernardine's fervorinos on the Name, we can see that there was a much deeper reason than the purely pragmatic: Bernardine had a deep and fervent desire to set the Name of Jesus always before him, and for all men to gaze on the Name that is above all other names. Finally, weak and infirm, Bernardine set out for Naples in 1444, but died at Aquila whilst still en route. It was the vigil Office for the Feast of the Ascension and the Friars were chanting the words: 'Pater manifestavi nomen Tuum hominibus … ad Te venio'.

The great Franciscan's devotion to the written Name of God has its parallels in Judaism. Since the eighteenth century, most synagogues prominently display before the congregation a votive tablet known as a *shivviti*, so called from the opening word in Hebrew of Psalm 16, verse 8: 'I have set Yahweh always before me,' a verse which is always written on the tablet. In a manner reminiscent of the IHS monogram, the *shivviti* is a calligraphic design that provides a focus for prayer and meditation. It is a visible reminder of the presence of the Lord: many devout Jews will have a *shivviti* on a wall in their own homes as a visible reminder of the divine presence.

For us today, there is a great need to set the Lord always before us. We need reminders of the divine presence and of the need to sanctify the Holy Name. One simple and obvious way of doing this is to follow St Bernardine's example and to use the name as a visible icon. The Name of Jesus is a verbal and a written icon, not divine in itself but containing a 'presence' of the divinity. The Seventh Ecumenical Council taught that the honour which is paid to an icon passes over to the prototype and, even mere pertinent, the contemplation of the icon raises the eyes of the mind to both the ineffable and to that which is represented.

Traditionally, the icon made of wood and paint has been regarded as a sacramental of presence, and the whole point of the icon is that it differs essentially from that of which it is the image. The icon manifests the invisible but does not incarnate it. The image leads to the contemplation of the invisible, a contemplation which is by way of affirmation and then negation, for the invisible is contemplated in that which is represented. The sacred humanity of Christ is the icon of his divinity. The Name 'Jesus' is not divine in itself but Christ is present in his Name in the same way that he is present in the Scriptures, and since the Person named is divine, the Name shares in the holiness of Jesus himself to an appropriate extent.

Through faith, the Name of Jesus is a corridor or a window through which Christ is present to the Christian, although not substantially as in the Eucharist. The Name is thus a meeting place, a place of encounter between the heart of the believer and the Heart of Christ. It is because of the incarnation of the Son of God that the ineffable Name of God can now be 'imaged' in human words, the Name of the Incarnate Word, Jesus. Not only has the Son made himself visible in the flesh and lived with men, He has a name that is both audible and can be written by man: YESHUA, IHS, JESUS.

In an Angelus address given on 22 December 1996, Pope John Paul prayed that Mary may 'put on our lips and impress on our hearts this most holy Name from which comes our salvation'. He spoke the following words to the assembled people:

> Jesus! This name, by which Christ was known in his family and among his friends in Nazareth, exalted by the crowds and invoked by the sick during the years of his public ministry, calls to mind his identity and mission as Saviour. In fact, 'Jesus' means 'God saves'. A blessed name, which also proved to be a sign of contradiction, ended by being written on the Cross in justification of his death sentence. But this name, in the supreme sacrifice of Golgotha, shone forth as a life-giving name in which God offers the grace of reconciliation and peace to all mankind.

To look at that Name with love is to stand at the foot at the Cross and to receive the spirit of grace and supplication.

---

1 Alfred Edersheim (1825–1889) was born in Vienna to Jewish parents. As a young man, he was converted to Christianity. Although dated and at times marred by a certain polemical spirit, his *The Life and Times of Jesus the Messiah* remains a wonderful compendium on the Jewish social and religious background to the Gospels. In spite of certain inaccuracies and theological shortcomings, Edersheim succeeds as few others in vividly evoking the world to which Christ belonged in his earthly ministry.

2 It is interesting to note that all that remains of the traditional relic of the *Titulus Crucis* (the Title of the Cross) brought to Rome from Jerusalem by St Helena in the fourth century consists of the words 'of Nazareth' in Latin and Greek engraved backwards as in Hebrew or Aramaic, as indeed it may have been written by a Jewish scribe used to writing from right to left. Only the lower half of the Hebrew inscription remains at the top of the inscription, and can indeed be read as '*HaNozr*', the Nazorean/Nazarene. In a remarkable and thought-provoking book, *The Quest for the True Cross* (London, 2000), Carsten Peter Thiede and Matthew D'Ancona contend that the fragment is not a risible medieval forgery, an obvious fraud, but quite possibly of first-century Palestinian origin. The authors also cite the work of a Jewish scholar, Shalom Ben-Chorin, who worked on the basis of

the Greek text in John 19:19, and reconstructed the Hebrew as '*Yeshu HaNozri V_eMelek HaYehudim*', that is, 'Jesus the Nazorean and King of the Jews', four words whose initial letters were *Yod, Heh, Vav, Heh*, the Tetragrammaton, the holy name of YHWH itself (*op. cit.* pp. 105–6). The relic is preserved in the Church of Santa Croce in Gerusalemme in Rome. What is often overlooked by sceptical scholars who dismiss such claims on the *a priori* grounds that such things cannot be, is the very natural human desire to preserve significant items as a link with the past. Similarly, it is perfectly probable that St Helena's discovery of the Holy Sepulchre in 326 was made possible by a continuous oral tradition in the Jewish Christian community as to its precise location. Given that the fact of the empty tomb was a central point in Christian apologetic, it would be extremely unlikely that its site had been forgotten, since it was the primary mute witness to the Resurrection.

# The Naming of the Animals

*I know all the birds in the sky, all that moves*
*in the field belongs to me.*   [*Ps* 50:11]

Buried deep within the mind of man, there remains still a long lingering remembrance of Paradise when man and beast were in harmony. We are haunted by a sense of the loss of that harmony, a yearning made all the more poignant by those precious moments of mutual recognition and affection between man and animal when it seems that the barriers between us are removed. One of the glories of our humanity is that we can feel a tender pity for the beasts and that they can feel trust for us – something, alas, in which they are so often deceived.

History and legend abound with stories of the love between man and animals. Going back to Homer, we think of Argus, the faithful hound, who awaited the return of Ulysses. After nineteen years, he heard his master's voice when Ulysses finally came back to Ithaca after his long years of wandering. Although Argus was too feeble to move, he wagged his tail, drooped his ears and no sooner had he set his eyes on his beloved master than he finally succumbed to death. Our dogs have names because they are very dear to us. They are not things or objects: they are individuals, personalities.

By giving animals names, we express our love for them, our recognition of their rights and our desire to enter into a relationship with them. The naming of animals, not only of dogs, is something human beings have been doing for a very long time. In so doing, whether we realise it or not, we carry on a tradition that goes back to the dawn of human history. Naming animals is part of what makes us human: it is one of the things that defines our human identity.

In *Genesis*, we read:

> Now the Lord God had formed out of the ground all the beasts of the field and all the birds of the air. He brought them to the Man to see what he would name them. Whatever the man called each living creature, that was its name. So the man gave names to all the livestock, the birds of the air and all the beasts of the field.   [Gn 2:19–20]

Man and beast alike are both made from the same material, formed out of the ground. 'Adam' is named after the ground, *'adamah'*, from which he is formed, but God breathes into his nostrils the breath of life and man becomes a 'living being' (a *nephesh*). God gives man authority over the animal kingdom and this is symbolised by man's naming of each species.

In the Yahwistic account of creation, God created the animals to relieve man's solitude. The creatures are brought before man that God might see what Adam 'would call them; and whatever the man called every living creature, that was its name'. As he stands before God and names the animals, man blesses God who has created all living creatures. He thus acknowledges that they are God's gift and exist to play their own part in God's loving plan of creation. Man is uniting himself to God's work in seeing that it is good. This is the true original blessing by which man acts as the priest of creation.

In man, creation finds a voice to praise the God who made all things and holds all things in being. United with the countless hosts of angels, who look upon God's splendour, man praises God's glory in the name of every creature under heaven. This voice of praise finds its supreme expression in the Mass, the prayer of Christ himself. When the great German mystic Blessed Henry Suso was asked what his thoughts were as he began the Preface, he replied that he was filled with visions and borne up to God, and through him all creatures:

> I place before my inward eyes myself with all that I am – my body, soul, and all my powers – and I gather round me all the creatures which God ever created in heaven, on earth, and in all the elements, each one severally with its name, whether birds of the air, beasts of the forest, fishes of the water, leaves and grass of the earth, or the innumerable sands of the sea, and to these I add all the little specks of dust which glance in the sunbeams, with all the little drops of water which ever fell or are falling from dew, snow, or rain, and I wish that each of these had a sweetly sounding stringed instrument, fashioned from my heart's inmost blood, striking on which they might each send up to our dear and gentle God a new and lofty strain of praise for ever and ever. And then the loving arms of my soul stretch out and extend themselves towards the innumerable multitude of creatures, and my intention

is, just as a free and blithesome leader of a choir stirs up the singers of his company, even so to turn them all to good account by inciting them to sing joyously, and to offer up their hearts to God. *Sursum corda*.[1]

By naming the animals, man becomes God's steward of creation; but this stewardship does not mean that he has a different origin from the animals. Both man and beast are made out of the dust of the earth. Both receive their being from God and, although man's dominion over the animals is absolute, it is not unbridled. The steward must answer to the Master. We are responsible to God for how we treat his creation because God's loving providence is not confined to man. As Our Lord tells us, even the sparrows that fall to the ground are not forgotten. The tender compassion of God extends to all of his works [*Ps* 146:9]. Here, the Hebrew word *rahamin* is used, the divine compassion and pity which, as we have seen, is especially linked with the name of YHWH. *Rahamin* is linked to the root *rehem*, 'womb', suggesting the depth of a mother's love for the child born of her womb.[2]

The fate of man and animals is linked. After the Flood, God remembered Noah and all the wild animals and domesticated animals that were with him in the Ark. He sent the wind to cause the waters of the Flood to subside. He told Noah to bring every living thing out from the Ark so that it could 'abound on the earth, and be fruitful and multiply on the earth'. The covenant made with Noah was not just with man, but a covenant with all that lives upon the earth. God set the rainbow as the sign of that covenant in the sky, where all creatures might see it. Nonetheless, the 'fear and the dread' of man are upon every living animal: this is the consequence of sin, the breaking of the communion that existed in Eden. Man is now given permission to eat meat:

> Every moving thing that lives shall be food for you. I have given
> you all things, even as the green herbs. [*Gn* 9:3]

A characteristic of the Genesis account of Paradise is the harmony between man and animal. Man has an atavistic desire to be able to converse with the animals and, again and again, we find the theme of humans speaking to animals in myth and legend throughout the world. A small child will want to talk to the animals. It is as if man has some racial memory of some terrible catastrophe in the past that severed the communion between man and animals. We long for its restoration.

The Scriptures show God's love and providential care for all his creatures. These are but a few references:

> He provides the beasts with their food
> and young ravens that call upon him. [*Ps* 146:9]

> You make springs gush forth in the valleys:
> they flow in between the hills.
> They give drink to all the beasts of the field;
> the wild asses quench their thirst.
> On their banks dwell the birds of heaven;
> from their branches they sing their song. [*Ps* 103:10–12]

> All creation unites in praising the Name of the Lord:
> Praise the Lord from the earth,
> sea creatures and all oceans,
> fire and hail, snow and mist,
> stormy winds that obey his word;
> all mountains and hills,
> all fruit trees and cedars,
> beasts, wild and tame,
> reptiles, and birds on the wing;
> all earth's kings and peoples,
> earth's princes and rulers;
> young men and maidens,
> old men together with children.
> Let them praise the name of the Lord
> for he alone is exalted.
> The splendour of his name
> reaches beyond heaven and earth. [*Ps* 148:7–13]

When St Francis of Assisi spoke of the beasts as his brothers and sisters, he was speaking the literal truth. Both man and beast alike are born out of the earth, called into being by God's love. The uniqueness of man lies in the fact that he alone is made in the image and after the likeness of God. But the animals are also made for the glory of God; they have their part to play in the kaleidoscope of God's glory that is the universe. The Word too calls them into being:

> Let all your creatures serve you, for you spoke, and they were made. You sent forth your spirit, and it formed them; there is none that can resist your voice. [*Wis* 7:20]

All join in the cosmic dance. As George MacDonald wrote:

> The bliss of the animals lies in this, that, on their lower level, they shadow the bliss of those – few at any moment on the earth – who do not 'look before and after, and pine for what is not' but live in the holy carelessness of the eternal now.[3]

A very archaic story, that of Balaam and his ass [*Num* 22], attributes to a creature a superior spiritual awareness than to a human, for it is the ass, not its master, that recognises the presence of an angel. The wise man will see that creation itself is a book of revelation charged with the glory of God, if only we had the eyes to see. The Wisdom literature is fond of telling us how the animals can teach us wisdom. Job asks, 'Who teaches us more than the animals of the earth, and makes us wiser than the birds of the air?' Even the ant points a moral to the sluggard. Solomon, the archetypal wise man, would 'speak of trees, from the cedar that is in the Lebanon to the hyssop that grows in the wall; he would speak of animals, and birds, and reptiles, and fish' [*Job* 5:22]. The question of the survival of creatures after death remains unanswered in Scripture. The Preacher asks, 'Who knows whether the human spirit goes upwards and the spirit of animals goes downwards to the earth?' [*Eccles* 3:21].

What is clear is that Scripture sees redemption of the animal kingdom as united to the redemption of man and the restoration of Israel. This is apparent in several of the prophets. *Hosea* speaks of a new covenant between man and the wild animals:

> I will make for you a covenant on that day with the wild animals, the birds of the air, and the creeping things of the ground; and I will abolish the bow, the sword, and war from the land; and I will make you lie down in safety. [*Hos* 2:18]

This is part of the betrothal between God and his People. Surveying the ruins of Jerusalem, *Joel* says even the wild beasts cry to God because the water brooks are dried out. The fire has destroyed the pastures of the wilderness, but they need not fear for the pastures will be green again.

It is in *Isaiah*, however, that we find the clearest references to the restoration; and this is linked to the coming of the Messiah:

> The wolf shall dwell with the lamb, and the leopard shall lie down with the kid, and the calf and the lion and the fatling together, and a little child shall lead them. The cow and the bear shall feed; their young shall lie down together; and the lion shall eat straw like the ox. The sucking child shall play over the hole of the asp, and the weaned child shall put his hand on the adder's den. They shall not hurt or destroy in all my holy mountain; for the earth shall be full of the knowledge of the Lord as the waters cover the sea. [*Is* 11:6–9]

God's love is steadfast, extending to the heavens; his righteousness is like the mountains, and his judgements like the great deep. He saves both man and beast [q.v. *Ps* 36:5–6]. The coming of the Lord will transform nature, and God will do a new thing:

> I will make a way in the wilderness and rivers in the desert. The wild beasts will honour me, the jackals and the ostriches; for I will give water in the wilderness, rivers in the desert, to give drink to my chosen people, the people whom I formed for myself that they might declare my praise. [*Is* 43:19–21]

Christ fulfils this prophecy when he goes out into the wilderness for forty days to be tempted by Satan. As Mark tells us, the Lord 'was with the wild beasts; and the angels waited on him' [*Mk* 1:13]. He is with the wild beasts as Noah was with the clean and unclean animals in the Ark for forty days. Christ in the wilderness with the beasts is the new Adam who ushers in a new age, and even the animal order hallows his Name. The Good News is for the whole of creation, not just for man, and the animal creation is part of the whole cosmos that yearns for the revelation of the sons of God.

In Eden, man had exercised the role of priest of creation by naming and blessing the animals. As a result of succumbing to the Tempter, the state of original blessing was lost and nature itself was wounded. Fallen man is no longer in harmony with living creatures: the fear and dread of man are upon them, and nature becomes wild. In the wilderness, the Second Adam is with the animals as Adam was with the animals in Eden, when he gave them their names. Christ's presence among them is the presence of the One who blesses and names, as the true High Priest. Through Him, all creation finds its voice and redemption is made present. His stay in the desert with the wild beasts is a sign that the coming of the Messianic age marks the dawn of Paradise regained.

The full significance of Christ's sojourn in the wilderness as a renewed consecration of the animal order becomes even more apparent if we reflect on the prayer of Christ. Our Lord prayed as a Jew and, as we have already mentioned, the characteristic form of prayer for a Jew to this day is the *Berakhah*: 'Blessed art Thou, O Lord our God, King of the universe, Who have ... [done whatever deed]'. From rising in the morning to sleeping at night, the *Berakhot*, the blessings, praise and thank God in all circumstances, no matter how mundane or commonplace, and invoke the presence of God.

It is perhaps important to note a subtle distinction of emphasis in the idea of blessing in Judaism and Christianity if we are to appreciate the true nature of a Jewish blessing. In Judaism, the primary emphasis is on the blessedness of God and giving Him thanks and praise. For the Christian, the emphasis is more general: 'blessing' includes the idea of prayer for a benefit of some kind, spiritual or material, together with the idea of setting a person or an object apart for a sacred purpose. Obviously, all of these elements are also present in Judaism as well, but the element of praise and thanksgiving is stressed more in a Jewish *berakhah* than in the more general concept of the Christian blessing. In fact, there is a good example of a Christian blessing modelled on a Jewish *berakhah* in the offertory prayers of the new Roman Rite of Mass – 'Blessed are you, Lord God of all creation, through your goodness we have this bread to offer'. All blessings are by their very nature eucharistic, in giving thanks to Him who is the source of all blessings.

The blessings or benedictions express the Jewish understanding of the role of Israel as a priestly people. For a Jew of the time of Our Lord, the world that God had made was never seen as divided into the supernatural and natural. Instead, the world was permeated by God's presence and power; it and everything in it was God's, but also God's gift to man to be affirmed, to become the subject of praise and thanks, to be consecrated anew to God by blessing. No matter how ordinary or mundane the activity or thing, from cock-crow in the morning to retiring at night, it was celebrated and consecrated by a blessing.

By the prayer of blessing, the 'sacrament of the present moment' is realised: God is discovered in the here-and-now. The *Talmud* lists some ninety-seven occasions during the day when a blessing should be pronounced and gives an appropriate formula for each. Every blessing begins with the prescribed formula 'Blessed art Thou, Adonai, our God, King of the Universe'. A blessing must invoke both the Kingship and the Name of God for, as the *Tractate Berakhoth* 40b states, 'any benediction that is without mention of *ha-Shem* (i.e. the Name) is no benediction at all'. This affirmation of God as King is known as *'shem u'malkut'* – the Name and the sovereignty.

The Rabbis taught that when we pray we should do so in the awareness that the Divine Presence (the *Shekhinah*) is before us. These blessings renew the work of Adam in naming the animals, expressing and recognising the true meaning of things as coming from God and charged with his glory. It is a way of prayer which is essentially an affirmation of God's action, of acceptance of God's will in creation and in every aspect of life, that God may declare the greatness of his Name and his will be done on earth as in heaven. The *berakhot* express our wonder and thanksgiving at the blessedness of God.

In the Benedictions, man is the priest of all creation and as God's steward offers to him in his Name the praise of the universe. The *berakhot* sought the perpetual remembrance of the God who created the world, the God of the Covenant, and reflected an awareness of the whole of life as shot through with his glory. The Jew was called to give glory to God, to become once more the Adam who had named the creatures of God and thus directed them to their Creator anew. Every event, every object, every person was a summons to thanksgiving, turning man towards God, man who is essentially *homo adorans*.

By invoking the Name over creation, man says 'Amen' to God's creative plan and consecrates the whole of the universe to God. In the wilderness, the Son of Man consecrates the animals to his Father. It was necessary that when the Son of God came as the second Adam, he should renew the work of Adam who had named the wild beasts: all creatures are once again to become 'clean'. As St Paul tells us, Christ is 'the first-born of all creation; for in him all things were created ... all things were created through him and for him.' [*Col* 1:16].

Our prayer is a sharing in the mystery of his death and resurrection, and a saying 'yes' to the gift he offers us of his own prayer. Christ predicted the destruction of the old Temple and the rebuilding of a new Temple, his Body, a Temple not made with human hands. This new Temple is still in process of being built up, with ourselves as the living stones. Not only man, but also the whole of creation is involved in this building-up of the Temple until Christ is all in all. This is a part of what the Kabbalists refer to as the *tikkun olam* – the restoration of all things. To use a parallel from the mysterious world of quantum theory, where the observer changes what is observed by the very act of observation, so in pronouncing the Name over all things and in discovering the Name in all things, the created order itself is once more directed to God and shares in the redemption. St Paul points to the cosmic perspective:

> The creation waits in eager expectation for the sons of God to be revealed. For the creation was subjected to frustration, not by its own choice, but by the will of the one who subjected it, in hope that the creation itself will be liberated from its bondage to decay and brought into the glorious freedom of the children of God. We know that the whole creation has been groaning as in the pains of childbirth right up to the present time. [*Rom* 8:19–22]

St James tells us that God gave us 'birth by the word of truth, so that we would become a kind of first fruits of his creatures' [*Jas* 1:18].

Cast out of Paradise, Adam wept and creation mourned, for Man was created to be the link between the earthly and the spiritual world. The Greek Fathers speak of man as a glass through which the divine might shine into the earthly world, so that the earthly, elevated with the divine, might be freed from corruptibility, and transfigured. Man had been called to name the created order, to accept the world from God, to bless and offer it to God in one great act of thanksgiving. Creation fell silent and man lost the gift of naming. But this was not the end of the story, only its beginning.

The coming of Christ, his death and resurrection, and the sending of the Spirit, bridge the abyss. As the Second Adam, Christ sums up all things in himself and offers them to the Father in the unity of the Spirit. In Him, the eternal Passover of all things to the Father has been achieved and is now being realised. We are saved not by being taken out of the world that God has made, but in it and with it. Man is the first fruits, but the harvest is the whole of creation: the salvation not just of mankind but of creation itself is rooted in the Name of Jesus. Although the ox and the donkey do not appear in the Christmas narrative, the traditional image of them in the stable offering their mute adoration is not the fruit of sentiment but a genuine Christian *midrash* on the text. The association between the animals and the manger comes from *Isaiah* 1:3 – 'The ox knows its owner and the donkey its master's crib'. Our Lord links the two in his rebuke to the scribe:

> The Lord then answered him and said, 'Hypocrite! Does not each one of you on the Sabbath loose his ox or his donkey from the stall, and lead it away to water it?' [*Lk* 13:15]

The Risen Lord tells the Apostles to preach the good news to the whole of creation, and that in his name 'they will pick up serpents and if they drink any deadly thing, it will not hurt them'. What Christ is saying is not to be taken in a literal sense, for it is far deeper than that. It is a promise that in his Name there will be a transformation of the relationship between man and animal.

By blessing the world in the Name, we carry on Christ's priestly work and discover Him at the heart and centre of all things. Creation itself is seen as an epiphany reflecting the hand and glory of its maker. As Gerard Manley Hopkins wrote: 'The world is charged with the grandeur of God'[4]. This leads to a profound sense of holy awe and reverence at God's creation and for the glory of the animal kingdom. The doors of perception are cleansed. We become aware that the healing oil of his Name has been poured out over all of creation – the grace of the Holy Spirit – and discover that 'there lives the dearest freshness deep down things'. The anonymous Russian Pilgrim expressed it beautifully:

> And when with all this in mind I prayed with my heart, everything around me seemed delightful and marvellous. The trees, the grass,

the birds, the earth, the air, the light seemed to be telling me that they existed for man's sake, that they witnessed to the love of God for man, that everything proved the love of God for man, that all things prayed to God and sang his praise. Thus it was that I came to understand what the *Philokalia* calls 'the knowledge of the speech of all creatures', and I saw the means by which converse could be held with God's creatures ... Everything drew me to love and thank God; people, trees, plants, animals. I saw them all as my kinsfolk, I found on all of them the magic of the Name of Jesus.[5]

This restoration of communion between man and animals is often manifested in the lives of the saints. We think of St Cuthbert's penitential exercise of praying at night standing in the sea with the water up to his shoulders. When he emerged from the sea at dawn, the otters would breathe on his feet to warm them and try to dry them by rubbing them with their fur. Nearer our own time, there is the strange and magnetic figure of the Russian Orthodox St Seraphim of Sarov. In him, a contemporary of Jane Austen, the Desert Fathers lived again. Seraphim spent his last years in the vast solitude of the Russian forests, surrounded by large numbers of animals, including bears and wolves, who came to be fed by him and share his company. The ecstatic prayer 'My Jesus' was ever on his lips and in his heart.

The harmony between man and beast to which the lives of so many saints bear eloquent witness foreshadows the world that is to come. It is not surprising therefore to note that the holy icons frequently depicted a transfigured animal creation as having its place in Heaven itself. St John the Evangelist heard 'every creature in heaven and on earth and under the earth and in the sea, everything in the universe, cry out: "To the one who sits on the throne and to the Lamb be blessing and honour, glory and might, forever and ever" ' [*Rev* 5:12].

We are reminded of the words of the ecstatic prayer known as the *Nishmat kol hai* – the 'breath of all living' – a prayer that in its earliest form Our Lord himself may well have known. The first part of the prayer dates from the days of the Temple, and the second part from the first century before the coming of the Messiah. This is the prayer used to this day to open the synagogue service every Sabbath morning. It is a pure paean of praise, worthy of a St Francis of Assisi. Praising the Lord whose Name is the source and fount of all that exists, it calls on the whole of creation to give thanks to God's Name, whilst acknowledging man's complete inadequacy to thank God as he should:

> The breath of every living being shall bless thy name, O Lord our God, and the spirit of all flesh shall continually glorify and exalt thy memorial, O our King ... Though our mouths were full of song as the sea, and our tongues of exultation as the multitude of its waves, and our lips of praise as the wide-extended skies; though our eyes shone with light like the sun and the moon, and our hands were spread forth like the eagles of heaven, and our feet were swift as hinds, we should still be unable to thank thee and to bless thy name, O Lord our God and God of our fathers, for one thousandth or one ten-thousandth part of the bounties which thou hast bestowed upon our fathers and upon us.[6]

By invoking the name of Jesus over creation, we share in Christ's work of binding up the ancient wounds of our world and bringing all things again to the springtime of Eden. A new song of praise has begun on earth that shall never end:

> Alleluia, alleluia. My mouth shall sing the praise of the Lord, and let all flesh bless his Holy Name. Alleluia. I will extol Thee, O God my king: and I will bless Thy Name, O Jesus, for ever, yea, for ever and ever. Alleluia.
>
> [Feast of the Holy Name: Tridentine Missal]

---

1  Quoted in V Gollancz (ed.), *A Year of Grace*, London, 1950; p.69.

2  The law against causing unnecessary pain to any living creature is known in Hebrew as *Tzaar Baalei Hayyim*. Rabbi Louis Jacobs comments in an article on the subject of compassion: 'Compassion is to be extended to animals as well as to humans. It is strictly forbidden to cause unnecessary pain to animals. There is a Talmudic rule (*Gittin* 62a),

still followed by pious Jews, that before sitting down to a meal one must first see that the domestic animals are fed. The *Midrash* remarks that Moses proved his fitness to be shepherd of Israel by the tender care with which he treated the sheep when he tended to the flock of his father-in-law.' Louis Jacobs, *The Jewish Religion: a Companion*, Oxford, 1995. The *Midrash* says that when Moses was tending Jethro's flock, he noticed a little lamb break away on its own and he went after it. He found the lamb quenching its thirst in a brook. Moses said to the lamb that if he had known that it was thirsty, he would have taken it in his arms and carried it to the brook. At that point, a voice spoke to Moses from heaven, 'As thou livest, thou art fit to shepherd Israel'.

3  Quoted in C S Lewis (ed.), *George MacDonald: an Anthology*, London, 1970; p. 114.

4  Gerard Manley Hopkins, *God's Grandeur*.

5  R M French (tr.), *The Way of a Pilgrim*, London, 1972; pp. 31, 106.

6  *The Authorised Daily Prayer Book of the United Hebrew Congregations of the British Commonwealth of Nations*, London, 1962; p. 173.

# The New Name

*I will give you the treasures of darkness and hidden riches*
*of secret places, that you may know that I, the Lord, who*
*call you by your name, am the God of Israel.* [*Is* 45:3]

Ask a young child why he is called by his name. The whole mystery of
names will be in the answers you receive. The child will tell you that he
has his name because his parents gave it to him. This is the first great
truth. Our names are gifts given to us by others. Although we can change
our name in later life, we can never change the fact that our first names
were given to us by someone else. We receive our names from our parents
as we receive life from them. While the child is still in the womb, parents
will discuss what name to give to him or her when born. This giving of
the name marks birth and new life. It is also a sign of a child's complete
dependence on his parents. Names are pure gifts. They are about knowledge
and love, and, for the Christian, the giving of the name is a sacred rite;
for, as the Catechism teaches, 'In Baptism, the Lord's Name sanctifies
man, and the Christian receives his name in the Church' [2156].

If you pursue the question about why the child is called 'John' or
'Mary', or whatever the name may be, you will find the second great
truth. Once you get beyond questions of personal preference, likes and
dislikes in names, the baffled child will finally answer, 'I am called John
because I *am* John'. Intuitively, the child grasps a truth that an adult can
easily overlook. The name is the person and the person is the name. As
the *Catechism* teaches, our names are sacred because they are icons of the
person.

In a very real sense, we are our names. They do not simply identify us.
We are present in our names. They manifest who we are. By our names,
we affirm our uniqueness and individuality as persons and people
acknowledge us as such. Our name signed at the foot of a document is our
legal seal, our word, and our testament. When we reveal our name, we
open ourselves to others, and to be without a name is to be cut off from
human society.

To seek to destroy a name is to seek to destroy a human being. At Auschwitz and the other camps, those selected to work as slave labourers rather than for immediate gassing were tattooed with numbers: the destruction of their names foreshadowed the destruction of their bodies. By blotting out the names of their victims, the SS began the process of eliminating them from humanity and life itself. In many parts of Europe under Nazi control, even the names of the Jewish dead on tombstones were erased. Ever since the establishment of the State of Israel, researchers at the Holocaust Memorial, *Yad Vashem* ('a hand and a name'), have sought to gather the names of all those who perished. Humanity revolts at the obscenity of the dark evil that would eradicate our names.

Those who love know intuitively the truth of names. The lover will want to hear the name of the beloved said over and over again. They will want to talk about that person and want to hear their name spoken. They will bring the conversation around to that topic just to hear the name of the one they love. Our love songs are often little more than rhapsodies on names. A young mother will cradle her new-born child and keep repeating his name. Names are special, almost magical. They express what lies in our heart but cannot be put into any other words. All of us die with names carved on our hearts, the names of those we love. At our deathbed, the priest will exhort us to call on the name of Jesus. Drawing on the infinite treasury of the merits of Christ, his mother and the saints, the Church grants a plenary indulgence to those who die with the Name of the Lord on their lips. As we breathe forth our soul, we call on his Name.

Instinctively, we react against the dehumanising process by which bureaucracy seeks to identify us by number instead of by name. On purely logical grounds, this method may indeed be much more convenient. The young John will discover that he is but one of a legion of Johns. Even the surname will not remove all ambiguity. Even so, identification by number repels us as inhuman, as destructive of the warmth of flesh-and-blood relationships. To reduce man to a number is to deny him his humanity. We are not numbers. We are human beings with names and our names are not mere labels: they are the symbols of the deep core of our being.

Although we cannot overestimate the importance of our names, there is still something provisional and transitory about them. There is a gap between our own names and us in ourselves. They are written on water. Names are not necessarily unique to us. Our parents gave them to us at a time when we were only just setting out on our pilgrimage, and our names cannot tell the whole truth about us. They make us present in the hearts and minds of other people but they do not sum us up. We may acquire other names on that journey, religious names or nicknames, for example, and our given names are not and cannot be the final word about us. Sometimes those names will have been chosen with great care and at others for more flippant reasons. All sorts of motives are at work in the process by which we are joined to a name: family tradition, religious devotion, fashion, a liking for a particular sound, a desire to please a relative or friend. Normally, that name will remain with us all of our lives. We are indeed truly wedded to the names our parents gave us – but it was an arranged marriage. Like the gift of life itself, the gift of our names comes before our ability to consent.

The names we receive from our parents are only a shadow of the names that one day we shall receive from God. He is the true giver of names. He has received his own ineffable Name from no other. That Name is the divine essence Itself, infinitely transcending all of creation and one with God's being. No human language can contain the Name that sustains the whole universe. He who is himself his Name is the source of all names, for he is the source of all being. The names that God gives us reveal what we are in our innermost self. God alone can give us our true names because he knows us – for we are a mystery to ourselves. Our moment of judgement comes when we hear the name that God gives and then, with an absolute certainty, we recognise that name as our own.

In the Apocalypse, Our Lord speaks of this ultimate name:

> To him who overcomes I will give some of the hidden manna to eat. And I will give him a white stone, and on the stone a new name written which no one knows except him who receives it. [*Rev* 2:17]

The Rabbis taught that when the Messiah came in the last days, he would again give the gift of manna, the angelic bread that had nourished the people of Israel in the desert. Christ fulfilled this prophecy when he gave us himself as the Bread of Life, the pledge of eternal life. The gift of the white stone is linked to the gift of manna and refers to the day of our judgement. In the ancient world, white stones were often used as tokens of admission to a banquet. A special guest at a feast would be given a white stone with his name or a message written on it. Juries used white stones to signify acquittal and people gave them as tokens symbolising happiness and joy.

The idea behind the Biblical image is clear. The one who conquers will receive the right to enter the messianic banquet; the banquet of heaven itself, and the name on the stone is a sign of their recognition and welcome by the Messiah. That name is the perfect and final statement of who and what we are. It is the name that the Lord will confess before his Father, and the name inscribed in the Book of Life.

The time will come when we hear our own innermost name, the name that expresses utterly and totally who and what we are in the mind of God. The giving of that name will indeed be the moment of truth when the veil will be taken from our eyes and we will see ourselves as we truly are. That name will be the ultimate statement of who and what we are – it will be the name by which God called us even in the womb, the name that has been with us all our lives and which, until then, we will never have heard. Then we shall immediately know that it is our true name. It will be a name that will be utterly unique to us as individuals, and our judgement will be an apocalyptic moment, for apocalypse is the taking-off of the mask and the removal of the veil.

No one has ever expressed this truth better than George MacDonald, the nineteenth-century Scottish writer whose work helped lead C S Lewis to the Christian faith:

> The true name is one which expresses the character, the nature, the being, the meaning of the person who bears it. It is the man's own symbol – his soul's picture, in a word – the sign which belongs to him and to no one else. Who can give a man this, his own name? God alone. For no one but God sees what the man is, or even, seeing what he is, could express in a name-word the sum and harmony of what he sees. To whom is this name given? To him that overcometh. When is it given? When he has overcome. Does God then not know what a man is going to become? As

surely as he sees the oak which he put there lying in the heart of the acorn. Why then does he wait till the man has become by overcoming ere he settles what his name shall be? He does not wait; he knows his name from the first. But as – although repentance comes because God pardons – yet the man becomes aware of the pardon only in the repentance; so it is only when the man has become his name that God gives him the stone with the name upon it, for then first can he understand what his name signifies. It is the blossom, the perfection, the completion, that determines the name; and God foresees that from the first, because he made it so; but the tree of the soul, before its blossom comes, cannot understand what blossom it is to bear, and could not know what the word meant, which, in representing its own unarrived completeness, named itself. Such a name cannot be given until the man is the name.

God's name for a man must then be the expression in a mystical word – a word of that language which all who have overcome understand – of his own idea of the man, that being whom he had in his thought when he began to make the child, and whom he kept in his thought through the long process of creation that went to realise the idea. To tell the name is to seal the success – to say, 'In thee also I am well pleased'.[1]

The giving of the white stone marks the completion in time of God's workmanship. Then we shall receive our own true name that, unlike all the other names that we have borne, is not written on water, but a name that is eternal and imperishable (cf. *Is* 56:5 – 'I will give them an everlasting name that shall not be cut off'). We shall learn our own true name that is written on the palms of God whose hands were nailed to the cross: 'See, I have inscribed you on the palms of my hands; your walls are continually before me' [*Is* 49:16].

The reference to our names' being written on God's hands carries with it a wonderful association. In the *Shema*, the Jews were commanded to bind upon their hand words which included the Name of God. They came to interpret these words literally and, by the time of Our Lord, the practice of wearing *tefillin* (phylacteries) was common. *Tefillin* are two cube-shaped black leather boxes containing words of Scripture, including the *Shema*, with leather straps so that one box may be worn on the head and the other on the arm which is traditionally seen as the equivalent of the hand.

When today a Jewish man puts on *tefillin* before morning prayer, he will wrap one strap three times around the middle finger, saying the beautiful words of *Hosea* 2:19–20:

> I will betroth you to me forever; yes, I will betroth you to me in righteousness and justice, in loving kindness and mercy; I will betroth you to me in faithfulness, and you shall know the Lord.

Just as God's Name is to be on our hand, so on God's hand, our own true name is written as a perpetual remembrance in the mind of God. When that name is revealed to us on the white stone, then God will give us 'treasures out of the darkness, and riches that have been hidden away'. Then indeed we shall know that he is the Lord, the God of Israel, who calls us by name [*Is* 45:3]. This giving of our true name is the moment of mystical marriage: that moment of restoration and redemption when, at last, after our long exile, we come home.

The Apocalypse sees the final perfection of the Christian and the final consummation of all things as inextricably linked. Written at a time of bitter persecution, the *Apocalypse* is very much a call to Christians not to grow weary but to be ready to suffer for the sake of the Name, to hold fast to the Name even unto death. To those who have been victorious, to those who have hallowed the Name of God, the Messiah will give also another name: the Name which is above all names, the name of the Lamb of God himself. The one who overcomes will be a pillar in the Temple of God and Christ promises:

> I will write on him the Name of my God and the name of the city
> of my God, the new Jerusalem, which comes down out of heaven
> from my God. And I will write on him my new name [*Rev* 3:12].

The redeemed will see the Lamb of God face to face and his name will be written on their foreheads.[2]

In all of this, there is a great comfort and consolation. For each of us, God has a meaning and a purpose. He calls us each by name, the name which in the mind of God expresses the totality of our being, the name uttered by God with a love beyond all imagining. In *Isaiah* we find these words:

But now, thus says the Lord who created you, O Jacob, and he who formed you, O Israel: 'Fear not, for I have redeemed you; I have called you by your name; You are mine. When you pass through the waters, I will be with you; and through the rivers, they shall not overflow you. When you walk through the fire, you shall not be burned, nor shall the flame scorch you.' [*Is* 43:1–2]

If we are to discover what being a person means, then we must look at God himself, for we find our own names in the Name of God. No one is a number in the eyes of God. He calls each one of us by name and in his own most Holy Name. In this exchange of love, we discover who and what we are, the very meaning of our lives and our eternal destiny, our own true name.

---

1 G MacDonald, *The New Name in Unspoken Sermons: Series One*, Whitehorn, California, 1997; pp. 71–72. The great Flemish mystic, Bl John Ruysbroeck wrote in his book *The Sparkling Stone* in a similar mode on the new name: 'Behold, this is the sparkling stone which is given to the God-seeing man, and in this stone a new name is written, which no man knoweth saving he that receiveth it. You should know that all spirits in their return towards God receive names; each one in particular, according to the nobleness of its service and the loftiness of its love. For only the first name of innocence, which we receive at baptism, is adorned with the merits of our Lord Jesus Christ. And when we have lost this name of innocence through sin, if we are willing still to follow God, especially in three works which he wishes to work in us, we are baptised once more in the Holy Ghost. And thereby we receive a new name which shall remain with us throughout eternity.'
2 In *Exodus*, the high priest had the words 'Holy to the Lord' on his forehead on a plate of gold [*Ex* 28:36–38] and the *Urim* and *Thummin*, the stones he wore on his breastplate, had the Name of Yahweh inscribed upon them. The seal on the foreheads of the redeemed recalls the *sphragis*, the signing with the + or x on the forehead at the baptismal anointing. According to *Ezekiel* 9:6, the *Tau*, the last letter of the Hebrew alphabet (X in the archaic form of that alphabet) is the mark of Yahweh on the elect. The Hebrew *Tau* is the symbol of the Name of God. Q.v., 'They shall see his face, and his name will be on their foreheads' [*Rev* 22:4] and 'Then I looked and there was the Lamb standing on Mount Zion, and with him a hundred and forty-four thousand who had his name and his Father's name written on their foreheads' [*Rev* 14:1]. In the *Odes of Solomon* (see end of Chapter One), Christ descends into the depths of Sheol and saves those who acknowledge him as Saviour by placing his Name upon their heads [*Ode* 42].

# On the Jesus Prayer

*But you, O God the Lord, deal with me for your name's
sake; because your mercy is good, deliver me. For I am
poor and needy, and my heart is wounded within me.*
[*Ps* 109:21–2 (NJV)]

Perhaps the most subtle and dangerous temptation facing us today as we
come to prayer is that we bring with us all the unconscious pre-suppositions
and mental baggage that we bring to so many other things. We approach
prayer as consumers, forgetting that all prayer must be that not our will
but that of the Father be done. To be a disciple of Christ is to respond to
his call to take up one's cross and follow after him. There is no road other
than the royal road of the Cross. The fundamental commandment is to
love God with all of one's mind, heart and soul, and one's neighbour as
oneself. This presupposes a life centred on communion with the whole
Christ, his Church, Head and Body, a life nourished by the Holy Scriptures
and sacraments of the Church.

Anyone who sees the way of the Name as a spirituality aimed at the
attainment of some form of 'heightened spiritual consciousness' by using
the Name as a mantra is totally mistaken. This is what we might term the
New Age approach, which is simply a bogus spirituality centred not on
the living God but on ourselves, a spirituality laced with Gnostic elitism
and usually utterly divorced from any idea of an ethical dimension to
prayer. There are no shortcuts to mystical union with God and, at the end
of the day, we are examined in love, not in the spiritual 'experiences' that
we may or may not have had. If we love him, we must obey his command-
ments: the test of our love of the God whom we cannot see is our love for
our neighbour whom we can see.

There are many ways to use the Name of Jesus in prayer. There is
great freedom here. For some, simply repeating his Name with love and
attention is enough, and this is the way advocated by Lev Gillett in his
book *The Jesus Prayer*. As long as the Name is not seen as some form of
talisman and there is no attempt to seek after spiritual 'signs and wonders',
such a way is, of course, perfectly safe. But the majority tradition of Eastern

Christendom is that we should set the Name of Jesus in the frame of the Jesus Prayer: 'Lord Jesus Christ, Son of God, have mercy on me, a sinner'.

In a few words, the Jesus Prayer expresses the essence of the faith of the Church. The Prayer is the most marvellous summary of the whole Gospel and it is a prayer that says everything. The first half of the Prayer is an act of adoration, a loving acceptance of the whole economy of salvation and of God's tender and merciful love for mankind. We unite our voice with the voice of all creation in proclaiming that 'Jesus is Lord' – Adonai, the One who was, who is and is to be, risen and glorious, the King of the Universe and whose Kingdom we wish to reign in our hearts. He is 'Jesus', the Lord who is Our Saviour and our salvation, and the 'Christ', the longed-for Messiah, the Son of David and the anointed One whose Name is like oil poured to heal all our wounds. Then we affirm that he is 'Son of God', the eternal and incarnate Word. We are directed to the reciprocal and everlasting flow of love that is the Trinitarian life of God. Through the Son and in the unity of the Spirit, we go to the Father and are drawn ever deeper into the divine life which is the eternal sabbath, the abyss of silence, the source and goal of all.

The second half of the Prayer is a plea for mercy, a plea which is not only for forgiveness but for God's gracious self-communication of his own divine life: God is mercy, and to pray for mercy is to pray to partake in that divine life – to be established as sons in the Son. The Prayer is our cry for mercy, for salvation from our sins: mercy is God's faithful and compassionate love, the divine pity itself. Our prayer is grace in return for grace, an expression of our *teshuvah* or 'turning' to God, the return home from the long exile; for the gates of repentance are always open, since the Lord our God is rich in mercy. We pray the prayer of the tax collector and, in asking for mercy, we are asking Jesus to be a Jesus unto us, for Jesus is the Mercy of the Father made flesh. To pray for mercy is to pray to share in the divine life itself, for we are sinners who need a Jesus. The Prayer concludes with the 'me, a sinner', for that is what we are, creatures who need a Jesus.

The essence of the Prayer lies in the fact that it contains the Name of Jesus: it is emphatically *not* some form of Christian mantra but a prayer addressed to a Person from whom the Prayer derives its efficacy. With regard to certain physio-psychological practices that are sometimes mentioned in books on the Prayer, linking the words of the Prayer to breathing, one thing can be said with absolute certainty: their practice is quite unnecessary. All of the great Eastern spiritual masters regard them as purely secondary, at most as an optional aid, never to be attempted without a spiritual guide. In the twentieth century, when spiritual guides with sufficient knowledge are rare, such techniques are best not attempted. They involve the risk of very real physical and spiritual dangers to which the beginner might easily fall prey without expert advice – and here 'expert' refers to someone who has progressed far in the wisdom and love of God, not to someone who has done a crash course in yoga. There is no shortcut to contemplation and no other way than the way of the Cross:

> Do not become attracted by inner sweetness: without the Cross it
> is unstable and dangerous. Consider everyone to be better than
> yourself. Without this thought even a worker of miracles is far
> from God.[1]

God can indeed raise a soul to contemplation suddenly and within a short period of time if he so wills, but this is not his normal way of acting: the Jesus Prayer is the work of a lifetime and not a means of arriving at an instant mysticism. The truly charismatic life is the ordinary, day-by-day life of the Christian, nourished by God's grace in word and sacrament, and it is in this life that the Jesus Prayer may find a place, not as a means of escape but as a means of participating more knowingly and more deeply in the mystery of Christ. In Salinger's novel *Franny and Zooey* a bored young student seeks in the Jesus Prayer a romantic way of escaping the tedium of her social life. It is only when she is led to discover Christ in a woman dying from cancer that she discovers the true nature of prayer and that it is not an exercise in spiritual escapism centred on the selfish acquisition of 'religious experiences'.

How then are we to say the Prayer? First, we must remember that it is not a technique but a prayer. An Orthodox layman, Tito Colliander, gives the following excellent counsel:

> Repeat (the Jesus Prayer) aloud, or only in thought, slowly,
> lingeringly, but with attention, and from a heart freed as much as
> is possible from all that is inappropriate, but also such things as

every kind of expectation or thought of answer, or inner visions, testings, all kinds of romantic dreams, curious questions and imaginings. Simplicity is an inescapable condition, as is humility, abstemiousness of body and soul, and in general everything that pertains to the invisible warfare. Especially should the beginner beware of everything that has the slightest tendency to mysticism. The Jesus Prayer is an activity, a practical work and a means by which you enable yourself to receive and use the power called God's grace – constantly present, however – within the baptised person – in order that it may bear fruit.[2]

This warning against spiritual illusion and gluttony is in perfect accord with the doctrine of St John of the Cross, the safest of all spiritual guides, whose teachings can seem so stark and uncompromising, but are so only to the false ego mired in all its selfish cravings and attachments. We must die to self so that the adopted son of the Father may arise like a phoenix from the fire which has consumed all self-will, to become in actuality what we are already in seed as the result of baptism: the glory of God, man fully alive.

Let us begin then by saying the Prayer, quietly, calmly, with trust and perseverance, with sorrow for our sins, with love and with adoration, recognising that no one can say 'Jesus is Lord' except by the Holy Spirit. At this stage, the Prayer is said aloud or silently by the lips. St Paul exhorts us to 'pray without ceasing', and we begin with the prayer on our lips, praying it over and over again at all times and places. The beauty of the Prayer is its very simplicity: it becomes our constant companion. This is an arduous task for, although described as oral, this stage involves mental prayer, since the mind must be fixed upon the meaning of the words said by the lips, upon the sovereign presence of Jesus and the nothingness and need of man.

If, with God's grace, we persevere, the Prayer goes deeper within us, acquiring a rhythm of its own, and gradually, our minds become more and more centred on the Prayer. The mind finds itself repeating the Prayer and it is no longer necessary for it to be said aloud or silently by the lips. Then comes the final stage, the prayer of the heart, when, through the gift of God's transfiguring grace in the Spirit, the prayer enters into our heart, the deep core of our being, as we enter ever more deeply into the presence of him whose Name is our joy and through whom we go to the Father in the transforming gift of the Holy Spirit.

Since all prayer is a participation in Christ's Passover, the Jesus Prayer has to be seen in the context of the prayer of the Church, the prayer of the risen and glorified Christ, Head and members. All true prayer is the prayer of Christ, and Christian prayer is the acceptance of the proffered gift of Christ's own prayer. In prayer, the Head and members speak with a single voice: 'Erunt duos in voce una'[3]. As Francis Durrwell comments:

> If it is true that everything finds its unity and completion in the paschal Christ, that everything else was created for him (*Col* 1:16), it is also true that all things are made for prayer. For the redeeming Christ is a temple, his pasch is a prayer, and our prayer is spoken in that temple and that pasch.[4]

There can never be any opposition between subjective and objective piety, since all true prayer is that of Christ's Mystical Body, and through every true prayer something happens in that Mystical Body. It is the Mystical Body, the Church herself, who prays in that prayer, for the Holy Spirit lives in her, pleading for us in the innermost depths of our heart in a way that transcends all words. Consequently, the Jesus Prayer cannot be set over and against liturgical prayer as if there were some opposition between the public and private prayer of the Christian. Above all, liturgical prayer is prayer 'in the Name of Jesus' and the Jesus Prayer is directed at accepting the redeeming Christ as our prayer by a deeper union with him.

What gives the Jesus Prayer its special power is the fact that it contains this all-powerful Name: the power comes from faith in Jesus, for the Prayer does not work mechanically or divorced from the Christian life. The essential thing is to stand consciously in the presence of Jesus, with sorrow for one's sins and in humility of heart, with faith, hope and charity. Bulgakov wrote of the light of the Name of Jesus illuminating the universe, and observed that:

> Not only is God invoked by this Name, but he is already present in the invocation. This may be said, of course, of every name of God, but it is especially true of the divine and human Name of

Jesus, a Name belonging to both God and man. In short, the Name of Jesus, present in the human heart, gives it the power of deification which Our Redeemer accorded us.[5]

At the dawn of Israel's history, God promised that 'in every place where I cause my Name to be remembered I will come to you and bless you' [*Ex* 20:24]. The promise of God is irrevocable as are all his promises. Through baptism, we have become a Temple of God wherein his Name pitches its tent and dwells among us. We pray that we may always remember that his Name is in our hearts, asking that he may hallow his Name in us and that we in our turn may hallow his Name with all our heart, and soul and might. Then we shall discover the blessing of his presence and how he has always walked with us on the way even when we knew him not.

As I come to the end of this book, I know that there is so much more that could be said and so much that has been poorly said. When we contemplate the wonders and the glory of the Holy Name, we are like children standing on the beach and looking out with wonder at the vast ocean that stretches out before us. We shall never cease to explore the ocean of God's Name and of his love for us. In Jesus, we find the abyss of the Father's love for us, the infinite treasure of his mercy and the boundless joy of his Spirit.

The words of the 'Father of English prose', Richard Rolle, are as true now as they were in the fourteenth century and may fittingly conclude this book:

> If you wish to be on good terms with God, and have his grace direct your life, and come to the joy of love, then fix this name 'Jesus' so firmly in your heart that it never leaves your thought. And when you speak to him using your customary name 'Jesu', in your ear it will be joy, in your mouth honey, and in your heart melody, because it will seem joy to you to hear that name being pronounced, sweetness to speak it, cheer and singing to think it. If you think of the name 'Jesus' continually and cling to it devotedly, then it will cleanse you from sin and set your heart aflame.[6]

1  The Nun Magdalina, in T Ware (ed.), *The Art of Prayer: an Orthodox Anthology*, London, 1996; pp. 128–9.

2  T Colliander, *The Way of the Ascetics*, London, 1960; pp. 108–10.

3  St Augustine, *In Ps. Lxi*, 4; *Patrologia Latina*, 36 (370).

4  F-X Durrwell, *In the Redeeming Christ*, London, 1963; p. 191. The quotation is from St Francis de Sales, *Sermons*, Vol. III, p.49; Editions d'Annency, 1897, Vol. 9.

5  S Bulgakov, *The Orthodox Church*, New York, 1935; p. 170.

6  Richard Rolle, *The English writings*, translated, edited and introduced by R S Allen, London, 1989; p.173.

# SELECT BIBLIOGRAPHY

*In this book, I have used the New King James Version (NKJV) of the Bible, unless otherwise stated. The NKJV is an extremely faithful translation that seeks to preserve all of the information in the text, whilst presenting it in good literary form. Some modern translations are so intent on making the Scriptures 'more accessible' to the modern reader, that at times they paraphrase rather than translate what is actually contained in the sacred text. As a result, some references to the 'name' of God in the sacred text disappear in the English translation. For the deutero-canonical books, I have used the New American Bible.*

Anonymous, *The Way of a Pilgrim*, trans. R M French, London, 1972.

Anonymous, *The Pilgrim Continues his Way*, trans. R M French, London, 1973.

Balz, Horst & Schneider, Gerhard, *Exegetical Dictionary of the New Testament*, Grand Rapids, 1991.

Besnard, A-M, *Le Mystère du Nom*, Paris, 1962.

Bialik, H Y & Ravnitzky, Y H (eds.), *The Book of Legends: Sefer Ha-Aggadah*, New York, 1992. Legends from the Talmud and Midrash.

Bolshakoff, Sergius, *Russian Mystics*, Kalamazoo, 1976.

*Catechism of the Catholic Church*, London, 1999 (revised edition).

Cohn-Sherbok, Dan, *The Jewish Faith*, London, 1993. An excellent introduction to the Jewish faith for the general reader.

*Encyclopedia Judaica* (CD-Rom Edition), Jerusalem, 1997. The most comprehensive, authoritative resource on the Jewish world.

Farb, Peter, *Man's rise to civilization as shown by the Indians of North America*, London, 1969. Contains some very perceptive comments on the relationship between language, thought and culture.

Hammer, Reuven, *Entering Jewish Prayer: a Guide to Personal Devotion and the Worship Service*, New York, 1994.

Hausherr, Irénée, (Trans. Charles Cummings), *The Name of Jesus* (*Cistercian Studies Series*, 44), Kalamazoo, 1978. The definitive academic study of the development of devotion to the name of Jesus, especially in the East.

Jacobs, Louis, *The Jewish Religion: a Companion*, Oxford, 1995. Presented in dictionary form, this work covers all of the main beliefs, practices and personalities of the Jewish faith.

Kittel, Gerhard & Friedrich, Gerhard (eds.), *Theological Dictionary of the New Testament*, Grand Rapids, 1964–1974. The standard and indispensable New Testament dictionary.

Matt, Daniel C, *The Essential Kabbalah: the Heart of Jewish Mysticism*, San Francisco, 1995. An annotated anthology and translation of some key Kabbalistic texts.

A Monk of the Eastern Church [Archimandrite Lev Gillet], *The Jesus Prayer*, revised edition with a foreword by Kallistos Ware, Crestwood, New York, 1997. A classic work on the Jesus Prayer.

Rudgley, Richard, *Lost Civilisations of the Stone Age*, London, 1998. Includes material on 'Proto-World'.

Scholem, Gershom, *Major Trends in Jewish Mysticism*, New York, 1961. The definitive work on Jewish mysticism.

Scholem, Gershom, *On the Kabbalah and its Symbolism*, New York, 1965. A thematic approach to the history of the Kabbalah.

Steinsaltz, Adin, *The Essential Talmud*, New York, 1977. Not an abridgement of the Talmud but a practical guide to the Talmud by a great Talmudic scholar.

Steinsaltz, Adin, *A Guide to Jewish Prayer*, New York, 2000. A definitive guide by the leading Talmudic scholar.

Swietlicki, Catherine, *Spanish Christian Cabala*, Columbia, 1986. Deals with the whole question of the 'Christian' Kabbalah and its traces in the works of Luis de Leon, St Teresa of Avila and St John of the Cross.

*The Orthodox Study Bible*, Nashville, 1993. The New Testament and Psalms in the New King James Version. A beautifully produced Bible with copious study aids, articles and an excellent commentary written from the perspective of Orthodox Christianity, and thus in almost complete harmony with that of the Catholic Church.

Ware, Kallistos, *The Power of the Name: the Jesus Prayer in Orthodox Spirituality*, Oxford, 1974. Perhaps the best short introduction to the Jesus Prayer in English.

Ware, Timothy (ed.), *The Art of Prayer: an Orthodox Anthology*, London, 1966. The compiler, Fr Chariton, was *Igumen* (superior) of the Russian Orthodox monastery of Valamo.

# Glossary of Key Terms

*Alenu* (It is our duty)  Prayer at the end of a service proclaiming the greatness of God.

*Amidah* (standing)  A prayer consisting of eighteen blessings.

*Aron Hakodesh* (Holy Ark)  Alcove cupboard in a synagogue containing the Torah scroll.

*Berakhot*  Blessings.

*Brit-milah*  Covenant of circumcision.

*Kabbalah* (received tradition)  Esoterical and mystical Jewish tradition.

*Kaddish* (holy)  Aramaic prayer of praise.

*Kedushah* (holiness)  Biblical verses chanted by the cantor during the 'Amidah'.

*Kiddush ha-Shem*  Sanctification of the Name.

*Masoretes* (Tradition)  Refers to scribes who fixed the traditional text of the Scriptures, especially by adding vowel sounds to show how the text should be pronounced.

*Mezuzah* (door post)  Parchment scroll attached to a door post.

*Minyan* (number)  Quorum of ten Jewish males over age of thirteen required for public acts of worship.

*Midrash* (searching)  Interpretation of the Scriptures taking many forms.

*Mikveh* (collection)  A ritual bath used for ritual cleansing.

*Mishnah* (teaching)  Codification of the oral law.

*Ner tamid* (eternal lamp)  Lamp constantly alight above the ark in a synagogue.

*Qahal*  The assembly of the people.

*Sefirot*  The ten divine emanations from God in kabbalistic thought.

*Septuagint*  The Greek translation of the Bible, dating from the third century BC.

*Shavuot* (weeks)  Festival of Weeks celebrating the wheat harvest and giving of the Law.

*Shekhinah* (dwelling)  The presence of God.

*Shema* ('Hear, O Israel...')  Prayer beginning with these words.

*Tanach*  The Hebrew Bible.

*Targum* (Translation)  Aramaic translations of the Hebrew Bible.

*Talmud* (teaching, study)  Name given to the two vast collections of discourses on the Law by the Jewish sages who flourished in the period 200–500 AD.

*Tefillin* (prayer objects)  Phylacteries: two black leather boxes containing the 'Shema' which are attached by leather straps to the left arm and upper forehead.

*Tetragrammaton*  The four-letter Name of God, i.e. YHWH.

*Tikkun olam* (repair, rectification of the word, all things)  Kabbalistic term for restoration of all things.

*Torah* (Teaching)  The five books of Moses and all of the oral law.

*Yad* (hand)  Hand-shaped pointer with extended finger used to mark the text when reading from the Torah.